Washing Cars & Wasting Time –
Misadventures at a Family-Run Car Wash

John C. Oliva

Orange Hat Publishing
www.orangehatpublishing.com - Milwaukee, WI

Published by Orange Hat Publishing 2013

ISBN 978-1-937165-40-6

The stories in this book represent actual events. The
details are accurate to the best of the author's recollection.
Certain names and identifying characteristics have
been changed to protect the privacy of those individuals
involved.

Printed in the United States of America

www.orangehatpublishing.com

John C. Oliva

This book is dedicated to Scott. I still miss you, bro.
I look forward to working a double shift with you at that big car wash
in the sky.

Preface

I like to think of myself as a storyteller. Undoubtedly this is a skill and hobby that I picked up from my father. As far back as I can remember, any family or social gatherings were marked with a small crowd gathered around my father as he told his many tales from the decidedly strange life that he lives. This even earned him the nickname of "The Guru." He still lives this crazy life, and he still draws a crowd telling his stories. In an unusually self-conscious demonstration of this phenomenon, my dad likes to retell the story of my mother complaining that he typically monopolizes the conversation at such gatherings: "You never let anybody else say a word! You talk the entire time!" Dad vowed to remain silent at a subsequent gathering, only responding when spoken to—like a "normal" person. He wore the resulting expanse of awkward silence as a badge of honor, a testament that his stories were the lifeblood of the conversation.

Many of the stories Dad tells are rather off the wall, with bizarre characters, absurd storylines, and unbelievable behaviors. In watching his delivery to an ad-hoc audience, I can often see the disbelief on their faces. I suppose I too did not initially know as a kid growing up in this environment just how much was fact and how much was embellishment. As life went on though, I had the opportunity to witness enough of these vignettes unfold in front of me to make me believe that most of the other madness were historical accounts.

From childhood through young adulthood, I am sure most of our friends and family suspected that I was born without a voice box. Living in the shadow of my father, I rarely got a chance to speak in such circles. And my sister, Jenni, too was born with "the gift of gab," as my father liked to call it, so even in the rare case when he was not around, Jenni was there to fill the silence. It was not until I started breaking away from my initial home life that I began to recognize that my father's habit had been passed down to me as well.

As a mid-thirty something myself now, I have had the opportunity to acquire my own little library of stories that I love to retell. Once a shy little boy who never made a peep in social gatherings, I have found that I seek out new circles of friends representing an always fresh audience. In my short life thus far, I have experienced my own cadre of weird circumstances, strange characters, and too-good-to-be true storylines. The depth and variety is such that one of my friends even suggested that I go out of my way to put myself into unusual circumstances just for the sake of getting a good story or two out of it. Maybe there is some truth to that. But I have finally taken to heart the often-heard compliment of "You gotta write a book some day about all of this stuff!" The book you hold in your hand is the product of such advice.

Amid all of my material, there is one collection of stories that I am finding ever more difficult to retell in the familiar oral tradition. From the age of about fourteen through the age of twenty-two (early high school through the end of college), I worked at my family's business: Speedee Car Wash, at the corner of Thirteenth Street and Layton Avenue on the south side of Milwaukee. At face value, this is a simple premise. But I find that the business, the location, the cast of characters were all so unique, that unless you were there, the stories cannot be properly retold in quick-fire fashion that my normal fare is accustomed to—believe me, I have tried. Geography and time have both taken me away from my car wash days. In retrospect, some of the stories were hard to believe at the time. Now it seems that if you did not experience the time and place first hand, the stories are hard to relate to, much less believe. However, my hope is that in the following pages I will be able to properly set the stage such that the great car wash stories can once again be dusted off and retold. If nothing else, I hope that you can go away from reading this with a few laughs and the satisfaction of knowing that the end of your childhood was not marred by working at "The Car Wash."

Entrepreneurship

It is an unremarkable neighborhood by most measures—the southeast corner of the intersection of Thirteenth Street and Layton Avenue on the southeast side of Milwaukee, Wisconsin. My family came to this corner in October of 1968. It was on this corner that my father, John F. Oliva, and my grandfather, Jack Oliva, assumed the Texaco franchise and established Jack Oliva Texaco Service. Perhaps "reestablished" is a more correct statement, as the business in various incarnations had already bounced around a couple of other locations in the Milwaukee Metro area before landing at this final spot.

Although a gas station is, on the surface, a straightforward business model, selling gas on the corner was just one of many ventures run out of the building. In addition to fuel sales and vehicle repairs, during various time periods the Texaco station also served as home base for a twenty-four-hour towing operation (light through heavy-duty), a snow plowing service for residential and commercial properties, and a moving truck rental center . . . just to name a few.

A single story can be used to provide a taste of the organized chaos that this organization became. I will begin with the disclaimer that, unlike most of the other stories you will read in these pages, I cannot claim to have witnessed the following events firsthand. Depending on the exact timing, which has been clouded throughout the decades of retelling this legend, specific dates have become vague at best. But given the constraints that frame the story, I was either a year or two out from being born, or I was a year or two on the other side of birth.

As the story goes, my father and one of his employees, called "Crazy Man" (a former helicopter mechanic from the Vietnam War), were closing up the station on a winter Sunday night. Across the street from the gas station and inset from the corner by one other property sat an apartment complex.

On this particular Sunday night, some new tenants were in the process of moving into the apartments, and there was not enough available parking onsite to park their rented moving truck for the night. The guy thus decided that he would park it in the gas station lot instead. So Dad and Crazy Man were still in the building when all of a sudden this twenty-four-foot-long moving truck landed in front of the two garage doors. Dad and Crazy Man walked out of the building to check out what was going on.

Dad: "Can I help you?"
New Neighbor: "Oh, no. I just need to park this truck here over night; we are going to unload it in the morning."
Dad: "You can't do that, you're blocking my two garage doors."
New Neighbor: "What's the difference? You're closed."
Dad: "Yeah, we're closed, but we do twenty-four-hour towing, and the tow trucks are behind those doors. If we get a call tonight, we'll be stuck inside the building."
New Neighbor: "Don't worry about it. I'm sure you're not going to get a call tonight. And I'll move the truck out of here before you open in the morning. Just don't worry about it."

And with that, he went across the street and disappeared into his new home. Let's consider some of the elements that contribute to this being a bad decision on the part of this young man. The two gentlemen he just pissed off moved disabled vehicles (including full-length and double-bottom semis) for a living. A twenty-four-foot-long moving van would be child's play for them. Furthermore, they also rented moving trucks themselves. Not only did they repair cars and trucks of all manner, but moving trucks in particular they knew like the back of their hands.

I am sure you can see where this is going. After a brief waiting period, Dad and Crazy Man went outside, slim-jimmed the door of the rental truck, and hotwired the truck to get it started. (Mind you, this was the early to mid 1970s. Locking steering columns and a lot of other anti-theft devices that have become the norm today were not commonplace, especially on commercial vehicles. And if the moving trucks of today are any indication, the truck was probably circa 1950 and had close to a million miles on it at the time.)

Once they had the truck running, one of them drove it down Thirteenth Street a couple of miles to the Ramada Inn. The other followed behind in another vehicle. The Ramada was one of those places that had a ridiculously huge parking lot . . . the likes of which has probably never been at capacity. So they parked the moving truck in the middle of the parking lot, where it did not look out of place, locked it up nice and tight, and called it a night.

The next morning, Crazy Man returned to the gas station to open up for the day. Lo and behold, the neighborhood's newest resident showed up shortly thereafter.

New Neighbor: "Where the hell's my rental truck?"
Crazy Man: "I don't know . . . I give up. Where is it?"
New Neighbor: "You saw me park it here last night!"
Crazy Man: "I did like you told us . . . I didn't worry about it. After we talked, I went home. It was gone when I got here this morning, so I assumed that you got it out of here just like you promised."
New Neighbor: "Well I didn't! What the hell am I going to do now?"
Crazy Man: "I suggest you call the police and report a stolen vehicle."

Eventually the Milwaukee Police Department's automotive detectives showed up and began to interrogate my father as to the whereabouts of the truck. "We think you're hiding it," the detectives told him. Dad explained that it was pretty hard to hide a twenty-four-foot-long truck. But he did pull out the pockets on his pants and jacket to show that it wasn't hiding in there either.

Detective: "What do you think happened? Do you think somebody stole it for parts?"
Dad: "That worn out thing? Only if they were dumb."
Detective: "Did they want to steal the contents?"
Dad: "Nah . . . they probably took it for a joy ride."
Detective: "Where would they leave it?"
Dad: "I'd park it in a large parking lot where trucks are usually parked. The airport parking lot or one of the hotels maybe."
Detective: "Yeah, OK. Don't quit your day job."

After answering their questions and letting them take a look around, the detectives disappeared.

Inevitably, a week later the police made a return visit to Jack Oliva Texaco.

Dad: "Hey, Kojak, did you find that truck yet?"
Detective: "No, did you?"
Dad: "Me? No. But I'm not looking for it . . . you are."

Dad had driven past the Ramada a few times in the past week, so he knew it was still there. And as another week went by, it continued to snow every day. The moving truck was forming a sizeable snow drift on it, and the Ramada snow plows just kept plowing it farther into the drifts. Eventually the detectives paid one more visit to the Texaco station to report a break in the case.

Detective: "We found that rental truck. The manager of

the Ramada called the rental truck company and told them that there was a truck on their lot that had a lot of snow piled on it . . . looked like it had been there for quite a while."

Dad: "So, the hotel manager found the truck . . . not you? Do you guys really get paid to do this? So, anyway, did the truck have a thousand extra miles on it? Or was it trashed like somebody had taken it for a joy ride? Was anything missing from inside?"

Detective: "Nope. It's in the same condition as when the kid in the apartments parked it here. And for that matter, it seems like the only additional miles on it were the two miles to drive it from here to there."

Dad: "I don't know what to tell you. A lot of strange things happen on this corner."

And that about sums it all up. A lot of strange things happen on the corner of Thirteenth and Layton. If that does not completely characterize my family's life and business in the neighborhood, it can only be stated more eloquently by the simple words on my dad's favorite workplace coffee mug: "Fuck 'em if they can't take a joke."

While all of the other ventures were run out of the gas station, the neighboring business owner, Otto Olson, approached my father with another proposal shortly after they set up shop on the corner. Olson operated a four-stall self-service coin-operated car wash named Speedee Car Wash that was just on the other side of the Texaco station's south property line. Olson had owned and operated the car wash for years at that point, and he was getting set to retire. He asked my father if he would be willing to act as manager of the wash while Otto remained the owner. Since Dad already worked right next door and lived across the street, he took the opportunity to make a few extra bucks. (My parents and older sister lived in apartments across the street from the car wash until a couple of years before I came into the world, at which point the family moved to a house back on the gas station side of Thirteenth Street.)

By today's standards, the original Speedee Car Wash was primitive. It was a corrugated steel building that consisted of four wash bays with a pump room in the center. Each stall was the drive through arrangement still common today— garage doors in the front and back, and cars pulled straight through. The walls of the building though were cruder than the common self-serve car wash of today, consisting of just sheet metal on a steel frame. The building was a rainbow of different colors from years of graffiti. In those early days, it was open twenty-four hours a day. Dad's managerial duties consisted mostly of repairing equipment that "customers" destroyed or stole the night before.

(On a side note here, keeping the business open 24/7 completely unattended seemed like just as bad of an idea then as it does now. Customers were able to lower the garage doors of the wash stalls and have their own little private room if they so chose. Dad tells me that on more than one occasion he found a couple using their private room for what one may expect at one o'clock in the morning. Why spend a few bucks on a trashy hotel room when you can use the comforts of your own car and the privacy of Speedee Car Wash? I can only imagine that the young ladies must have been very impressed by this evening out. The car wash was also used as a chop shop in the middle of the night for stolen cars. Dad would come to the business in the morning to find the remains of a stolen car after the thieves had removed all of the valuable parts from it.)

Between the initial move to Thirteenth and Layton at the end of 1971 and the end of the decade, things unfolded quickly. Grandpa died a few years after their move to the neighborhood. Dad went from managing Speedee Car Wash for Olson to buying it from him. Once Dad owned the car wash, he built a new auto repair facility right next to it and broke his ties with Texaco and the gas station on the corner. Also during this timeframe, my parents got married, had my sister and me, and moved into the house next to the new garage. (The house and car wash came as a package deal.) Jack Oliva Texaco Service was no more. The corner gas station building lay abandoned, but sitting next door was the new Oliva's Garage and the original steel shack Speedee Car Wash.

Progress was not to stop there though. During the year 1982, ground broke for an all-new structure to replace the first generation building on the same site. My father envisioned a whole new self-service car washing concept unlike anything the current market had to offer. When the new facility washed its first car in the summer of 1983, it was done to much fanfare in the self-service car wash world. My dad was a card carrying member of the International Car Wash Association and the Badger State Car Wash Association. The new Speedee Car Wash was a literal tour stop for the state convention the following year (kind of like a Parade of Homes, but for car wash geeks), and the business got some press in the automotive care industry magazines.

What made the new car wash so notable? For starters,

it was done on a grand scale. In lieu of the original tin shack's four wash bays, the new one offered thirteen. There were admittedly larger car washes in the country at the time, but not in Wisconsin. In addition to its size, the accommodations were indoor and heated—the perfect solution to washing cars in the harsh Milwaukee winters. Finally, almost defying common sense to the term "self-service car wash," the new business would be attended during all operating hours by at least one employee. Combine all of these innovative elements into one shiny new package, and the industry had not seen anything like it before. Our advertising campaigns at the time billed Speedee as "Self-Service Car Washing at its finest," and it was.

I literally grew up around the car wash. My family owned it when I was born, and I was six years old when the second generation facility had its grand opening. My parents have a picture of me with an impact wrench taking down the steel walls of the old building. In other pictures, my sister and I are painting the walls of the new building. We helped take down the old building and helped build the new one. Being around the car wash was just a part of our childhood.

I do not have a lot of distinct memories about the original Speedee Car Wash, but some of my earliest memories of it are from winters, when the floor would get completely iced over. As a family, we would occasionally spend time on the weekends chopping ice off the floors. It would get to be a half to a full inch thick across the entire floor of each stall. To my four- or five-year-old self, getting rid of all of that ice seemed insurmountable, like chopping the ice off of Lake Michigan.

Summers brought a completely different feel to the neighborhood. I remember spending time behind the original car wash a lot more than at the car wash itself. Between the parking lot of the original car wash and the neighboring drive-in restaurant, Martino's, our land was just kind of an unfinished, unlandscaped no man's land. It consisted of rocky soil with large weeds poking up through it. My sister and I took to calling this region "Wonderland," and even then the name seemed misleading. No matter, I remember playing out there, trying to dig in the dirt, or picking the weeds.

Of greater interest was that Martino's also had a miniature golf course that shared the back property line with Speedee Car Wash. This was an old-school putt-putt mini-golf course with primarily flat, concrete-lined putting greens. It had the occasional wooden obstacle, but mostly it was concrete and steel. No waterfalls, no moving hazards like windmills or spinning clowns, no giant caves like "adventure" golf courses would establish as the norm a couple decades later. But for all of its simplicity, I loved that golf course. My Auntie Toni worked at Martino's for a few years, and that earned my sister and me a free ticket to play the course. The owner, Mary Anderson, had a sweet spot for us and also let us play for free. My father and Mr. Anderson (insert your own Matrix joke here) did not get along, so Dad always encouraged us to refuse the free golf offers accordingly. But family feud be damned . . . we're talking free miniature golf! That course is so ingrained in my memory, I am sure I could sit down right now and draw a diagram of the entire layout—to scale.

The golf course predated at least the second generation of Speedee Car Wash, and in the end, it outlasted it too.

Once the new car wash was built, I found that there were advantages to being a kid with the state's largest indoor self-service car wash at your disposal. I could wash my BMX bike whenever I wanted—for free! And there were two speed bumps in the building to control traffic flow that made awesome bike jumps. OK . . . maybe those were the only true perks. But, nevertheless, my sister and I spent a lot of time in and around the business as we grew up. We played tennis against the back and side walls of the building, which frustrated my father, because we always hit balls too high, so they would land on the roof and roll into the rain gutters. After enough balls accumulated, Dad begrudgingly got up on the roof and shagged all of the balls out of the gutters. We could tell how long each had been up there based on how much yellow coloring had been retained. We also had a basketball hoop mounted on the south wall of the car wash, just outside the back door of Oliva's Garage. The basketball sometimes got stuck up on the roof too. What can I say? Sports have never been my strong suit.

As a result of how all of these events developed, we lived the first nine years of my life right next door to the business. The side of our yard bordered the parking lot of the garage and car wash. Even when we did move "away" in the summer of 1986, it was only down the block a couple hundred feet, so there was then another business between home and the car wash. This meant that the psychosis of the business did not have to go far to spill over into our home life. One such phenomenon was one for which I was convinced at the time was unique to Thirteenth Street. But since my years leaving the corner, I have been proven wrong. There is no nice way to put this: People shat on our building.

The first time this happened, I was still pretty young. When making the long fifty-foot walk to work one summer morning, Dad made the grisly discovery that somebody had defecated on the wall of the business facing our house. Not only was there human waste on the wall, but the perpetrator's soiled tidy-whities were also found near the crime scene.

This event had a profound impact on young John-John Oliva; a piece of my innocence was lost that day. But even now, after all of these years, that incident leaves many unanswered questions. What chain of events led to this man crapping on the side of a building? Was it a sudden urge or a lack of any other viable options? I do not subscribe to the notion that he found himself stranded in the middle of nowhere and could not find a proper toilet. There was a Clark gas station kitty-corner from us, and Martino's was right around the corner. Of the three options, I do not see how the brick wall ever became the preferred alternative.

And then there were the underpants that got left behind. How did he soil both the wall and his pants? If he shit his pants, how was there anything left for the wall? If he instead opted to squat against the wall, how did his drawers get involved? Unless he made the unfortunate decision of using his underpants in lieu of toilet paper? I will preemptively declare that if I ever find myself having just dumped on a business's wall and wiping my ass with my own shorts, I have definitely hit rock bottom.

This occurrence alone maybe is not that remarkable. What really drives the phenomenon home is that it happened *multiple* times. I can recall at least four different cases of this type of thing. The south wall got crapped on. The north wall got crapped on. An old abandoned vehicle behind the car wash got crapped on. And the crème de la crème . . . my father's minivan got crapped on. Could these have all been emergencies? Were some of them intentional payback for some perceived wrong that happened the day before in the car wash? Even at the conservative rate of four incidents in twenty years, if we assume that Speedee Car Wash was receiving a normal amount of such activity, the number of businesses in our neighborhood alone predicates that this goes on a lot more than my lifestyle leaves me privy to. Based on these numbers, on at least one night of any given week, one should be able to walk down Thirteenth Street and find somebody shitting on the side of a building.

We never had a name for this phenomenon. But just a few years back, I was listening to *Free Beer & Hot Wings* on Grand Rapids Radio. (If you have never partaken, I highly recommend the show. They are now getting syndicated around the country, and you can listen online from anywhere in the world.) One morning they made mention of this very phenomenon and termed it a "Poo-Poo Picasso." I don't know if they coined the phrase, but I have yet to come across something more descriptive of the genre. And the fact that they had a name for it proves that the car wash was not alone in being shat upon.

As we grew up, it just became a natural conclusion that my sister and I would work at the car wash ourselves when we came to age. Mom and Dad always told us that as long as our family had the car wash, Jenni and I would never have to work at a fast food restaurant when we were in high school. I heard this so often from my parents while growing up that teen fast food workers became demonized in my developing view of the world, much like people who drove foreign cars, patrons of cable television, and those unfortunate kids who had to attend public schools.

Jenni, who is two-and-a-half years older than me, started working as an attendant when she was a sophomore in high school, at age sixteen. I started a bit earlier in age, and I'd had odd jobs around the car wash, getting paid "under the table" as far back as I can remember: simple stuff like mowing the lawn, shoveling snow, or scraping globs of grease off the concrete floor with an ice scraper. But I became an official employee on the payroll at age fifteen. I then proceeded to spend the next seven years as an attendant at Speedee Car Wash, spanning the rest of my high school years and all of my college years. Although my sister started as an employee a year older than me, she attended a local school for her graduate work after college, so she was able to stay on for one year beyond her undergrad days, which I could not do. In the end, I think it was a photo finish as to who served more time at the wash.

In countless ways, my days at the car wash shaped me. I learned more in the stalls of Speedee than I have in any formal academic setting before or since. And my job at the car wash still holds the distinction of being the longest tenure I ever held. My time there forever changed the way that I view work, the general public, and my family.

Personnel

During the time period that I worked at Speedee Car Wash (roughly 1992 through 1998), it really was a family-run business. Other than a few random employees who did short stints through that same period, everybody on the payroll was related. We were a living example of the great American family-run business . . . for better or worse.

As a family, we were not too noteworthy, just your ordinary middle-class collection of people trying to navigate our way through life at the end of the last millennium. From an ethnic point of view, my father was from a purely Italian family and my mother was from a Polish lineage. That put us kids at a fifty-fifty blend. My cousin Scott who also joined us at the car wash had the same genetic mix, but his parents came from the opposite national origins as my own. The three of us kids always laid a greater identity claim to the Italian side of the family though, much to my maternal grandmother's dismay. This was probably just because being Italian seemed cooler to us. The Italians were reputed as having better food, there were fewer ethnic jokes targeting Italians, and if you claimed to your friends that you were Italian, you could also mislead them into believing that your family might have some shady tie-ins to the mob. Feeding in to our claimed Italian heritage was a small Italian restaurant down the block. It was short lived, but its presence spanned the same time period that we were all at the car wash. Ricobono's was run by the very Italian Ricobono family. Their family frequented our car wash, and we frequented the restaurant. To this day, it is the only restaurant where I had any name recognition. I could call and ask to make a reservation, and upon being told they were booked, I could mention that I was an Oliva and they would respond, "Oh! Why didn't you say so? Come down, we'll get you a table!" Between their all-you-can-eat crab leg and calzone specials, I consumed some mass quantities there, and my patronage may have had some blame in them going out of business.

We were also a decidedly Catholic bunch. My sister and I attended Catholic schools from first grade through high school, and she continued on through the end of her formal education. We never missed a Sunday Mass or a Holy Day of Obligation, and the major Christian holidays were a big deal in our house. Scott also had this Catholic upbringing, but to a lesser extent than in our household.

Like the above commonalities, and like with any job, our involvement at the business came to in part define us, so we all shared some common ground on that basis. Conversely, we each brought our own personality to the job, and in that sense, the business became defined by us as individuals. The following is a collection of short profiles of the main players who worked the stalls of Speedee Car Wash during the 1990s.

Name: John F. Oliva

Also Known As: Dad, Uncle John, The Owner, The Guru, The Old Guy, The Bearded Wonder, The Bearded Asshole, Asshole, Moses, That Homeless Lookin' Guy

Years at the Car Wash: 1972 through 1998. (Well, he's still technically there, he just uses the car wash building for "other purposes.")

Personnel File: Dad was the puppet master behind the whole Speedee Car Wash circus. He had very specific ideas regarding how he wanted his business to run, and he drilled those ideologies into all of us attendants so that we were all on the same page. Whereas many businesses trumpet the credo "The customer is always right," Dad's philosophy was more along the lines of "The customer is usually wrong. If somebody doesn't like something here, blow their ass out the back door and tell them that Super Wash is on Twenty-Seventh Street." With a boss like Dad, our biggest fear was being accused of being too easy on the customers and letting them walk all over us.

Owing to his cavalier business style, Dad was typically nearby and ready to fulfill the role of judge and jury in any disputes that arose between the car wash staff and its clientele. Dad is not a large man; he is probably only about 5'8" and weighs in at around 160 pounds. But what he lacks in physically imposing size, he more than makes up for in pure crazy. Through the years, Dad's appearance has been compared to that of Charles Manson, Ted Kaczynski, Moses, or a run-of-the-mill homeless man. Dad always said that he knew he looked as inviting as twenty miles of road construction, and he used his appearance to keep customers on edge and questioning what he might be capable of.

Despite Dad's unconventional appearance, I never saw him get physically violent with anybody—customers or otherwise. Growing up, Mom was the disciplinarian in our house. On the rare occasion that my sister or I did something that merited punishment (which seriously was not very often), Mom spanked us using her hand or her preferred weapon of choice: a wooden cooking spoon. I do not remember my father ever laying a hand on me, but Jenni likes to retell the story of Dad spanking her once with a small wooden block. Over the years, the event has become exaggerated—first a small block, then it was a larger block; eventually the legend grew to Dad railing on her with a two-by-four. In any event, my young sister's bloodcurdling reaction at the single hit deterred any more punishments from Dad, so it all got left to Mom.

Despite this peaceful aggression at home, I certainly saw him *threaten* violence a lot at the car wash. When a customer demanded "I want to talk to your boss!" or "I want to see the owner!" Dad did not even drop what he was doing to come meet with his public. If he was working on some plumbing in one of the pump rooms, he would emerge still carrying an eighteen-inch pipe wrench in his hand. Or, if he was under a car next door at the garage, he might walk over carrying a crow bar. For added measure, he would fluff out his long hair so that it kind of stood on end like Einstein's, just to amplify the crazy. To complete the picture, he typically approached the customer and said something like "Are you the one who wants to see the owner? Yeah, so what the fuck is your problem?" If the conversation did not end on its own momentum right there, it usually did not continue on for much longer.

One time Dad and Scott were working at the car wash on a busy day, and a disgruntled customer started beating on the machine in his stall with the spray wand. Dad walked over and demanded to know the problem. After explaining his complaint with the equipment, the customer told Dad that he was just going to continue to behave as he chose, and if Dad did not like it, he could call the police. Then he followed up with the taunt: "Go ahead; I know how quick the Milwaukee Police Department's response time is. I'll be long gone by the time they get here."

Dad turned to Scott and yelled, "Hey, Scott! Go grab me a piece of pipe from the north pump room!"

The customer asked, "What is the pipe for?"

Dad told him, "I'm going to start beating on you like you've been beating on my equipment. Go ahead, dial 911, the paramedics around here don't respond much faster than the police. But you'll be bleeding on your time, not mine. So you've got 'til three to get out of here. Two!!"

At that, the guy was last heard jumping into his car yelling, "What happened to 'one'?"

Dad took particular pleasure in not looking like most people expected the owner of a business to look. Apparently a lot of people assumed that even a small business owner should look like a Wall Street CEO. During one confrontation, a customer could not be convinced that Dad was the owner. So Dad told him to call the business's phone number during the week and ask to talk to the owner. When he actually did call the following week, Dad said, "Was that asshole with the big beard causing trouble and claiming to own the place again? Sounds like I need to have another talk with him!"

Dad's favorite disgruntled customer was one who told him he was going to call Dad's boss and "I'll get your minimum wage ass fired!"

Dad said, "Please do . . . put me out of my misery."

Some of Dad's most meaningful work took place outside of the confines of the car wash and garage buildings. In front of Oliva's garage, there is a two-and-a-half foot wall made of railroad ties. This was intended to serve as a barrier around the large gas meter that sits behind it feeding the car wash's boiler. But the railroad ties became the default place to converse with Dad when business in both the car wash and the garage was at a lull. Out on the railroad ties, we discussed all manner of life's issues. In this venue, Dad was as much mentor and guidance counselor to us car wash attendants as he was our boss. Father, Uncle, bouncer, counselor, repairman . . . Dad played many roles at the car wash.

Name: Scott Bonchek

Also Known As: Scrap, Booch, The Tall Kid

Years at the Car Wash: 1989 through 1997.

Personnel File: Scott was my cousin . . . my dad's sister's son. Scott was approximately five years older than me, putting his birth about a year before my parents got married. Since Dad was still living with my grandparents at the time Scott came into this world, they evidently spent quite a bit of time together during that first year, and a bond formed that lasted a lifetime. Dad and Scott were kindred spirits, finding common ground in being smart asses and clowning around. It was almost inevitable then that shortly after Scott could drive and entered the work force, he wound up at Speedee Car Wash. Scott did a short stint at a local home improvement store before joining the ranks of car wash attendants. But once he joined the staff of Speedee, he was in for the long haul.

Scott was drawn to all things dangerous and rebellious. He drove fast cars, collected guns, dabbled in making his own fireworks, listened to loud music, and didn't give a damn about school. But above all else, he just sought to have a good time. Every minute of every day was an opportunity to get a laugh. A classic Scott bit would occur at shift change, when he was taking over watch for one of the members of my family. He waited until we made the majority of the walk down the block back to our house. Then he would stand in front of the car wash and yell, for example, "Hey, Uncle John! Come back here! Hey, Uncle John!" (It happened to all of us eventually, some more than once.) Once he had the attention of his victim, he waved them back down as though they had forgotten something.

After Scott's pawn got back to the front of the building they would ask, "What's up? Did I forget something?"

Scott would smirk and say, "I wanted to ask you a question: What would you be doing right now if I hadn't called you back down here?" Then he would bend over in laughter. He never got tired of this stupid gag as long as he could trick one of us into it again. It was like working with Ernie, from Bert and Ernie fame.

In another scenario that was pure Scott, he was working one weekend, and Dad and I were headed to go pick something up with Dad's utility trailer. We were kind of running behind schedule, so on our way out of the neighborhood, Dad very quickly pulled the minivan and trailer across the front door of the car wash and yelled out his window, "Hey, Scott! Can you grab me a few bungee cords out of the north pump room and throw them in the trailer?" Scott started to casually meander to the pump room. Dad followed up his request with "We're in a hurry, can you please move slower?" Scott then started to mimic his slow motion running man and humming the song "Chariots of Fire." Dad turned to me and said, "Son of a bitch! That kid could fuck around all day long and never get tired of it!" Yes, that was an accurate summarizing statement of my cousin Scott.

I would estimate that Scott was about seventeen years old when he started working at the car wash; this put me at about twelve years old. Scott became the older brother that I never had. During summers, I wasted a lot of time just hanging out with him while he was on shift. When he was done working, we would continue to do random things together. Scott held the charm that he was kind of like a big kid. He was into many of the same activities that I was, but he had some money to fund them as well. We raced radio controlled cars, played video games, shot BB guns, and just drove around looking at girls. (We never talked to the girls, mind you. Scott was many things, but a lady's man he was not.)

Other than Dad, Scott was the longest-serving car wash employee we ever had. He eventually managed to graduate high school, and then he began attending a local community college. He toggled between having different majors (criminal justice, machinist, tool and die) and having no major. By the time Scott left the car wash after having served about eight years, he had also managed to earn a two-year degree in tool and die.

Most car wash employees had some idiosyncrasies, or they developed them as part of the job. Likewise, we all ate on the job out of necessity. Most often we were on shift alone, so there was rarely anybody to relieve us for a lunch break. Scott's favored on-the-job snack was Little Debbie Nutty Bars. He always had a box of these handy. More notable, though, was that during busy times, he had partially eaten Nutty Bars scattered around the building, so that when the urge struck, he could just grab a quick bite. On a busy day, he might have one half-eaten bar sitting on the small table near the pump room and another half-eaten bar at the other end of the building on one of the pylons near the back door. In between bites, the bars would sit unattended as people walked by, cars drove by, and car wash fluids flew everywhere. Possible contamination never seemed to faze Scott in the least.

A favorite Scott story from the car wash for both my sister and me came from a day that all three of us were working at the same time. I do not remember what circumstances led to this arrangement, but having three of us on the payroll at once was almost unheard of. Scott was working on some plumbing in the south pump room while Jenni and I were out tending to the customers. During a lull out on the car wash floor, Jenni and I ducked in to the pump room to see what Scott was up to. We found him busy at work, but his face had this steady stream of blood running down it, as though somebody had just hit him on the forehead with an ax.

    Jenni: "Dude, do you know that you're bleeding?"
    Scott: "I am? Where?"
    Jenni: "Ha ha. Very funny."
    Scott: "No, seriously, where am I bleeding?"
    Jenni: "Your face! Look in the mirror!"

    Scott walked a couple steps over to see himself in the small mirror that hung on the side of the boiler. In seeing his own appearance, he exclaimed, "Holy shit!" By this time, the blood was dripping past his chin and pooling on the floor. He had no idea what had cut him or why he did not feel the cut.

    As this incident demonstrates, Scott could entertain us without even trying. From the first day that Scott started working, he began spending more time around my family's home, and this gave us a glimpse into just how different his home life was from our own. For instance, he habitually walked into the living room in the evening after closing down the car wash and instinctively asked, "What movie are you guys watching?"

    We initially did not have cable TV or a VCR, so we were *never* watching a movie. From the sounds of it though, that's primarily what was on TV at his house. The best was when he walked in and asked what movie we were watching when we had on the evening news. Another curious reaction would happen when he showed up on Sunday evenings, the only day of the week that Speedee Car Wash closed at six p.m. instead of nine. I remember him asking, "You guys are having dinner again?" Sitting down at the kitchen table to eat supper every night was a completely alien concept to him.

    If you are wondering how Scott acquired the nickname "Scrap" while at the car wash, that was the product of a mutual misunderstanding and poor listening. One of the part truck delivery drivers who frequented Oliva's Garage next door introduced himself to Scott one day. Over the roar of the boiler and car wash pumps, the guy thought Scott said his name was Scrap. Scott, never having had the best hearing either, did not correct the guy, because he thought he was calling him Scott. The error was not discovered until the guy came in one day and asked me where Scrap was and I had no idea what we were talking about.

Name: Jenni Oliva

Also Known As: The Girl

Years at the Car Wash: 1990 through 1998.

Personnel File: Jenni held the obvious distinction of being the only female staff member of Speedee Car Wash for most of the time we all worked there together. Jenni started at the car wash at age sixteen, so right in the middle of her high school years. She attended an all-girls' high school and, later, an all- women's college. The high school required the girls to wear the cliché Catholic school girl uniform of a plaid skirt and button-down blouse. But Jenni was always the kind of kid to thumb her nose at convention as much as possible while staying within the letter of the law. She paired her uniform with insulated long underwear leggings under the skirt, men's navy surplus patent leather dress shoes, and an army surplus drab green wool overcoat. She also had a hairstyle whereby one side of her bangs hung low, completely concealing one eye. And to complete the picture, she had a so-called "rat tail" braid extending from her short haircut in the back, before such a feature went on to indicate other things. Her hair's style, length, and color changed like the weather during those years.

Dad learned that there were some advantages to having a teenage daughter. Even more so, one who was very tall, very thin, and had very long legs. He often sent us kids on part runs to pick up pieces for the cars he was working on in the garage. Depending on the establishment, it was not unusual for Jenni to be given complimentary parts just for being a girl and having "a nice smile," as she was often told. Being the token female attendant was a double-edged sword for her, depending on specific customers. Some people treated her nicer than they would us guys, while others saw her as a weak link and tried to take advantage of the situation. She did not let that crap fly though. She was pretty damn tough and held her ground even against the most obnoxious customers. Even so, I believe that she was the only attendant to receive monetary tips from customers for doing the same job the rest of us did. She was doing something right.

Although my sister shares my father's bright-blue Italian eyes, most customers did not recognize this resemblance and assumed Jenni was not part of the family. They occasionally attempted to confide in her and say things like "I can't believe you choose to work for that asshole."

Jenni would reply, "Oh, you mean my dad?" I think she really enjoyed those exchanges.

Jenni's course of study in college and graduate school brought an interesting dichotomy to the car wash. My sister successfully earned both bachelors and masters degrees in Catholic Theology while being employed at Speedee Car Wash. On slower car wash days, she was usually reading some assigned religious-based book while sitting outside the south pump room. Comparative scriptures, the synoptic gospels, Catholic social teachings . . . These were the likely topics you might find her reading about in the car wash. Most customers paid little mind to what we occupied our time with when not catering to their needs. But a few took note of Jenni's reading material and commented that they were surprised to see a car wash attendant reading such scholarly topics. In some ways though, what better study technique was there besides full immersion? The gospels relate countless accounts of Jesus surrounding himself with the lower ranks of his culture—tax collectors, prostitutes, and thieves. I think if Jesus walked the streets of 1995 Milwaukee, he would have felt right at home in the walls of Speedee Car Wash.

Most hints of sibling rivalry between Jenni and I disappeared by our car wash years, and the car wash itself probably played a role in that. We began to spend a lot of time together there; sometimes we were both working, sometimes only one of us was officially on the payroll. That dynamic carried into life in general, and we began to hang out a lot together outside of the car wash as well. Like soldiers at war or cops walking the beat together, I think that working together tended to be a bonding experience for all.

From our working days together, Jenni accumulated a lot of ammunition against me that she loved to hassle me about. For example, I have a deficiency in being able to accurately recognize people. She has often told me that I would not recognize her walking down the street if not given the context or foresight of knowing that I would see her that day. I used to think that I saw celebrities at the car wash, and, of course, it turned out that it was never really that person. Sure, in retrospect, it might seem implausible that MC Hammer would swing by during the height of his career to wash an ordinary Buick, but I swore it was him! What celebrities wouldn't take time out of their busy schedules to hit up Wisconsin's largest indoor self-service car wash? To this day, Jenni takes pleasure in teasing me about this. Like if we see some random tall, black guy, she might say, "Hey, John, I think that's Shaquille O'Neal over there. What do you think?"

Name: John C. Oliva

Also Known As: The Tall Kid . . . No, The Other Tall Kid

Years at the Car Wash: 1992 through 1998.

Personnel File: I was the baby of the crowd, both in terms of actual age and accordingly by being the one to officially start working at the car wash after Jenni and Scott had already been working there for a couple of years. Despite the age handicap though, I think I held the distinction of being the youngest person ever on the payroll.

As Dad liked to say, I was always the kind of kid who was afraid of my own shadow growing up. Tall, skinny, and socially awkward, I was the target of bullying and teasing throughout my school years beginning at a very early age. My social strategy by my high school years was to do my best to disappear into the woodwork and become invisible. If nobody noticed me, they could not pick on me was my theory. Being six-foot-three since the age of twelve though, shrinking into nothingness was never a foolproof strategy.

Scott and I shared a few physical characteristics, but I would not say that we looked alike by any means. We were both relatively tall and thin; Scott was probably only an inch or two shorter than me, and he was a bit heavier. We both wore glasses, and neither of us made it a point to shave with any regularity. But aside from those similarities, we barely looked related. Scott received the stereotypical dark Italian complexion and really dark hair, almost leaving him Hispanic in appearance. And he wore practically the same clothes to work every day—navy-blue sweatpants, a black T-shirt with either a beer company logo or rock band's insignia on it, and a Miller Lite baseball hat. I typically wore jeans, but the rest of my wardrobe fluctuated. But customers *always* thought Scott and I were the same person. As far as they could tell, the car wash had three employees—the old dude, the girl, and the tall kid. More often than not, this mistaken identity was a liability for me. Scott was more aggressive on every measure. As you might expect, he would piss off a customer during one visit, and they would return when I was working and seek to continue the squabble from the last time, of which I had no knowledge. On the days that Scott and I worked together, you could see the confusion on some people's faces when they finally recognized that there were *two* of us.

I credit my days at the car wash as being the catalyst to coax me out of my shell. By being an attendant, I no longer had the option of just becoming an unnoticed fly on the wall. This was a job that required a lot of conflict and confrontation. But I began to realize that the job catered to an ever changing clientele and, with that, the opportunity to reinvent myself with every new customer coming through the front door. They did not know me from eight years of grade school, and they did not come in the door knowing the pathetic reputation I had earned for myself in high school. I started down the road of becoming a stronger person. And on those days that I wanted to shy away from whatever situation was unfolding, Dad was there to hassle me. Hell, Jenni and Scott were there to give me a hard time too.

Looking back, I am not sure what really motivated me to work at the car wash. I can solidly say that it was not for the money. I recall that I rarely cashed my paychecks, so they would just pile up in my top dresser drawer. After I accumulated a few months' worth, Mom would complain that I was making her bookkeeping more difficult than it needed to be, and she would strong-arm me into cashing them. I think I wanted to work at the car wash more as being part of the club, being recognized as having grown up, and perhaps out of a sense of obligation to supporting the family cause. I was no longer content to sit on the sidelines while my sister, father, and cousin had all of these fantastic tales to tell from the frontlines of Speedee Car Wash.

While employed at the car wash, I pursued a bachelor's degree in mechanical engineering. I earned good grades in college and graduated near the top of my class. But it never came easy to me, and I spent an awful lot of time studying and doing homework. Between my commitments to homework and working at the car wash, I did not have the classic "college experience" that you see in the movies and on TV. I got so frustrated with my academics, I talked about dropping out of college all the time. During our railroad tie discussions in front of the garage, I lamented to my father about my despair at school. He could certainly relate, he earned his bachelor's degree in the same program at the same college, but he did it working *full* time, not this paltry little part-time car wash bit. I remember telling him that I should just drop out and become a garbage man. But he always encouraged me to stay the course and assured me that better things lay in the future.

The four of us constituted the main four staff members of the car wash. Like with any television sitcom though, the makings of a good story only come together when the unique set of personalities that make up the cast of characters find themselves in improbable situations. And at Speedee Car Wash, there was no shortage of improbable situations.

Perhaps it was merely a sign of the times, the car wash predating such things as eBay and Craigslist, but we had what I would deem to be an inordinate number of people come through the door trying to sell us random items. Some of them were literal door-to-door salesmen selling arbitrary gadgets and novelties. (I thought such activities had gone the way of the milkman and coal bins, but they still exist today. When my wife and I lived in Ionia, Michigan, we were shocked at how many people showed up at our front door trying to sell things.) Other would-be salespeople were less legitimate. They sold one-off items out of the back of their cars, evidently mistaking the words "car wash" on our sign for "pawn shop." I suppose that is an easy blunder to make. The wares that they were peddling were just as diverse as our customer base in general. Sporting goods, electronics, food . . . you name it. We had a guy offer to sell us some frozen shrimp. Ron, one of our very good customers, was given the opportunity to buy twenty pounds of potatoes from a fellow customer while at the car wash. My father bought a high-end VCR from a guy one time, and Scott also bought some electronics from this same individual. Shortly thereafter, one of this guy's friends told us that he had to "go away for a little while." The best car-wash-meets-swap-meet story that I have has to be the legendary crossbow story. Scott and I were both working on a busy Saturday in winter. Things were progressing like a usual busy day when a guy asked me if I would be interested in buying a crossbow. I told him I was not, but I knew who would be. I told Scott what the guy in the third stall on the north side was looking to sell. Before I had even gotten all of the words out of my mouth, the seller had a wad of Scott's money in his hand, and Scott was walking away more heavily armed than the average car wash attendant.

Scott's new toy sat in the south pump room for the remainder of our work day. When things slowed down, we drooled over and ogled the weapon. Like a kid on Christmas morning, Scott could not wait to give it a whirl. As soon as we ushered the final customer out the back door for the day, we locked all of the doors and set up a makeshift target on the back speed bump by flipping over a metal trash can and putting a cardboard box on top of it. We then walked to the other end of the building, where Scott loaded and sighted in his bow. He kind of crouched down low to the floor to steady his stance, and I stood beside him.

The rest all happened very quickly. I heard Scott hit the trigger and the arrow released. It sounded just like on TV. I also heard the arrow hit something—but, what? The cardboard box and trash can were still completely intact, unmoved. We walked to the back of the building and began looking around for the arrow. It proved to be hard to find, because only about an inch or two of the fletchings (aka "feathers") were sticking out of the back steel door, because the arrow had almost gone entirely through. Think about that for a moment. This thing packed enough punch that it propelled an arrow through an industrial-strength steel insulated door. The most startling part was that we opened the door to push the arrow back through, and one of the last customers of the day was still right outside the door drying his truck, only a matter of feet away from the projectile. This left us with the perspective that at least we did not kill the guy, but we were still going to have to explain to Dad why there was a new peephole in the back door. I told Scott it was all on him. *He* was the one who bought the crossbow, and *he* was the one who shot it inside the building, demonstrating his superior marksmanship. (He had missed the target by at least eight feet.) I was a mere innocent bystander.

We finished closing up for the day, emptied all of the coin boxes, and headed down the street like any other night. In typical Scott fashion, he was really casual, acting like nothing out of the ordinary had happened. As he was about to head home, he nonchalantly started a conversation with Dad.

Scott: "Hey, Uncle John . . . there is a small hole in the back door of the car wash . . . about a   quarter inch in diameter."

Dad: "The garage door?"
Scott: "No, the people door next to the back garage door."
Dad: "Does it go all of the way through?"
Scott: "Yup . . . all the way through."
Dad: "Do you know how that got there?"
Scott: "Yeah. I was trying to shoot a cardboard box with my new crossbow, and I missed."
Long, awkward silence.
Scott: "Ok, Uncle John, I'm gonna get going. I'll see you in the morning."
Dad (in murmured defeat): "Good night, Scott."

Archery and the car wash never seemed to mix well. (Who would have thought? It sounds like a match made in heaven.) My family had also acquired a traditional bow and arrow somewhere along the line. I think it may have come from my Aunt Josephine when we helped her move. Her late husband, Uncle Tom, was an avid hunter, and like a moth drawn to the flame, that bow too inevitably wound up at the car wash. My sister was working one day, and the two of us decided to practice our archery skills. The target was one of those black plastic witch's caldrons that people might decorate a front porch with at Halloween. (We probably found it in the trash.) We set the caldron on the car wash's rolling scaffolding in the first stall on the south side. This was an unfortunate choice, because that stall shared a wall with our father's office in the garage. Because of our great skill, we generated a lot more *tinks* off the wall than actual target hits. Dad walked around to our side of the building to see what the *tink tink tinking* was coming through the wall. It must have sounded like we were engraving our names into the block wall. When he saw what we were doing, he was not happy. The wall was all pot marked from each errant arrow hit. But, in our defense, we did not almost kill anybody, and none of our arrows made it all of the way through the wall.

There you have it: our crew . . . my coworkers . . .

mi familia. This was the set of major characters during the time I worked the car wash. There was another distinct set of attendants who worked the first six or seven years when the second generation Speedee Car Wash first opened. Like us, those guys worked there from about mid-high-school through their early twenties. And scattered throughout all of the years was an ever-changing cast of bit players who came and went, attendants who would last maybe a couple weeks, maybe a couple years. Some of them had names; some were around too short of a time to even earn that distinction. In the end, it was this complete collage of personalities and characters who made Speedee Car Wash the place that it became.

Headquarters

Of the four members of my immediate family growing up, my mother, Eleanor, was the only one of us who never worked at the car wash as an attendant. She on occasion came down while one of us was on shift so that we could have a brief food or bathroom break, but she probably never took over the reins for much longer than a fifteen-minute stint. But that is not to say that she never worked for Speedee Car Wash. On the contrary, Mom handled all of the day-to-day financial matters of the business behind the scenes. She reconciled the cash income at the end of each day, she took care of payroll, and she paid all of the bills to our suppliers and utilities. She did the bookkeeping for Oliva's Garage as well. Bear in mind, this was just her "side job." She worked full time at a series of different car dealerships through the years as a warranty administrator. Needless to say, between her actual job, her job with the family business, and taking care of most of the domestic duties around our house, Mom did not have a lot of time left for herself.

The car wash itself had no office space. Technically the garage next door had an office, but if anyone saw it, they would quickly conclude that it was no place to conduct business. My father has never thrown away a single piece of paper in his life. Important documents dating back to within the preceding decade are carried on his person in his "wallet." I am using the term wallet here in a very loose sense. Although it is made of leather and has some of the other defining characteristics of a conventional wallet, its contents tend to be less than normal. Money, identification, and an occasional credit card are carried in an alternate pocket wad. The wallet is reserved for scraps of paper with incomplete, incoherent notes, business cards from unknown people, and haphazard receipts. Not too long ago, I watched my father produce from his pocket filing cabinet his Vietnam War era draft card. He still walks in fear that his number is going to be drawn in the next Uncle Sam lottery.

Larger documents or paperwork dating farther back are kept in his garage office, on one of two desks. That is, I think there are desks underneath the piles. I don't think I have ever seen the structure under the papers, so it is possible that the piles of paper themselves are a full five feet tall rather than three feet of paper sitting atop a piece of furniture. Like arctic ice cores, one can in principle carve out a vertical slice of paper from the office and use it as a measure of history and the conditions that existed at that time.

Because this has always been the state of office space at 4726 South Thirteenth Street, the bulk of the business accounting activity took place down the block at our house. Mom usually had her filing system spread out over the dining room table and most often counted money in the living room. The dining room table had one distinction over the desks in Dad's office: We actually did eat at that table at least twice a year—normally Thanksgiving and Easter, but an occasional birthday and Christmas every few years also merited the table being cleared.

Growing up in the midst of this side of the business, we never gave a second thought at the time to the many abnormal things that became commonplace in our home. It was not until one of our friends would visit and serve as a litmus test of normalcy that we were alerted to the peculiarity of our own situation.

Chief among these elements were many things related to the cash flowing through our house. The car wash was by its nature an exclusively cash business, so at the end of each day, the attendant would empty all of the coin boxes from the thirteen car wash stalls into metal coffee cans. (I have gathered that it is unusual to know that a standard three-pound metal coffee can's capacity measured in quarters is approximately four hundred dollars.) On a slow summer day, a coffee can with barely an inch of quarters might show up at our back door at nine o'clock in the evening right after closing time. Busy winter days on the other hand might require two or three trips back and forth to carry five or six cans of quarters home. (A coffee can full of quarters is not particularly heavy, but it is awkward. There is little to grab onto, and most cans have a lip that runs around the bottom edge that tends to cut into your hands. And you do not want to be the idiot who drops a full can of quarters halfway to the house! A four hundred dollar quarter scramble in the dark, cold snow is no way to punctuate a long work day.)

Counting all of those quarters on a daily basis was no simple task. Not to mention that they were soaking wet—at the end of a busy day at the car wash, everything was wet. The coin vaults were right on the front lines of washing, so they caught their fair share of water. Not only did Mom not want to count all of those wet quarters, but our bank was opposed to taking in that quantity of wet money too. Early on, my parents contrived a method of drying the quarters by spreading an old towel on a similarly old cookie sheet, dumping the quarters on the towel, and sliding the pile into our kitchen oven. Since my parents always had gas ovens, they did not even need to turn the appliance on. The pilot light alone did enough heating and dehumidifying to dry a couple of sheets full of quarters when left in the oven overnight.

This drying practice resulted in the fact that at any given time during winter, our oven almost always had at least five hundred dollars worth of quarters sitting in it. I remember a couple of times when friends were over, if we were about to make a frozen pizza, we would just instinctively check the oven for quarters prior to turning it on. Our friends' jaws would hit the floor when we nonchalantly slid the cookie sheets of money out. To us it was nothing out of the ordinary. But we could tell that many of them were not accustomed to seeing large amounts of cash in any form, much less coming out of the oven.

Because of the car wash quarters, we also had an inordinate number of coffee cans around the house. (Coffee cans that are used to carry wet quarters do not last forever. The bottoms would begin to rust out, so we always had to keep a stock of replacements on hand.) We kept them stacked up on a ledge that ran along our basement steps. Here too, a mountain of coffee cans caught visitors by surprise, but I never thought twice about it. The first time I was asked, "Why do you have all of these coffee cans!?" I thought to myself, *How does your family carry quarters around?*

Once the quarters were in the house and dried, they still needed to be counted. In the very early days of the business, Mom counted all of the quarters by hand with brute force. You can imagine, though, that on a busy weekend, counting a few thousand dollars in quarters was a pain in the ass. So my parents' friend Ken, who was an avid woodworker, created a little device for Mom to count quarters. It was basically just a board that had a series of quarter-sized grooves cut into it. The width was such that each groove held ten dollars in quarters. This sped things up a bit, because then the individual quarters did not need to be counted. She could just fill the board up, and that equaled a known dollar amount. This device went through at least a couple of alterations with the accuracy of the width improving with each revision.

Our quarter-counting operation really hit the big time in the early nineties when Dad bought a used electric coin counting machine, the same type and quality that most banks had at the time. This investment had the biggest impact on lessening Mom's labor than any other purchase. With the coin counter in the mix, the dried quarters could be fed into the hopper and counted in a matter of a few minutes instead of hours. We then had an oversupply of coin-counting capacity, and Mom and Dad often ran the day's intake through the machine more than once to see how consistent the final tally was.

With that addition to the household, the first floor of our house was a minefield of abnormalities on display when company came over. Open the oven, and there may be a couple of cookie sheets full of drying quarters. Open the back hall closet, and it is occupied exclusively by an industrial-strength coin counter. The dining room was full of car wash paperwork. The front hall closet had a pile of bank bags in it. And Mom might be sitting on the couch counting big wads of paper money. It must have looked like we were running a drug operation out of our house.

The final leg of the cash flow in and out of our house was Mom's weekly trip to the bank. Mom would estimate how many quarters we needed to keep on hand in order to make change for customers. She kept meticulous records of each day's business on a calendar, noting weather conditions and cash intake. Based on the previous years' data and the current conditions, she could guess pretty well how much operating cash we needed to have in the form of quarters. But even with the quarters being re-circulated in this manner, the nature of things was still to, in general, accumulate our profits in the form of quarters. Thus, once a week, Mom took the extra accumulated cash to deposit at the bank, both in the forms of paper money and coins. For this transaction, she would forgo the standard coffee can transport method. The money was usually stowed in canvas bank bags, just like in the cartoons. To provide a little bit of camouflage though, Mom carried the bank bags in a repurposed Tweety Bird bag that my sister or I had gotten when we were very young when my mom and aunt had taken us to Six Flags Great America in Gurnee, Illinois. This must have been back in the days when amusement parks still sold quality merchandise in their gift shops, because the bag could have been mistaken for army surplus if not for the big yellow bird printed on both sides of it. One could safely carry a few bowling balls in the thick canvas bag, so it easily carried the bank bag payload. Each week on Saturday morning, Mom loaded up Tweety, mostly with quarters, and headed to the local bank to make the business's weekly deposit.

As a result of Mom's role in the business, she developed some unusual mental accounting abilities. As my wife would later observe, being an accountant / fiscal officer herself when she first met my mom: "Man, your mom is like a savant with the numbers!" Mom could balance a checkbook at lightning speed, she could estimate tax withholdings in her head, and she could mentally convert minutes to decimal equivalent hours. (Instead of having an official time clock to punch at the car wash, we tracked our time on a scrap of paper with handwritten time-in and time-out notations.)

An ability of Mom's that always impressed me was one that bordered on the super human. Prior to starting a family, Mom worked for the US Postal service in downtown Milwaukee at the main sorting facility. In these days, people sorted all of the mail manually, and that was Mom's job. This experience resulted in the entire zip code map of the greater Milwaukee area indelibly imprinted in her memory. Decades later, we could still fire at Mom "the corner of North Twenty-Second and Burleigh," and she would respond effortlessly with "53206."

Running Speedee Car Wash as a family in such close proximity to our home had other impacts on our lives. Somehow Dad convinced the phone company to allow an "off premise extension" to the business phone so that when somebody called the garage and car wash (they shared a phone number), there was an extension in our house that rang as well. From what I understand, this was pretty simple when the house and garage were only a matter of feet apart, but it became more complicated when our residence moved farther down the block.

This additional business phone line running to our house was a bit of a paradox. To this day, my father will not use an answering machine or voicemail. His mantra on the matter is always "If I miss a call, and it's truly important, they'll call back." Yet he can answer his business phone from home at any hour of any day.

The business phone in our house was kept in a back hall closet. (Yet another oddity hanging out in our house closets!) During normal business hours, it was standard operating procedure to ignore the phone in the closet when it rang, because somebody down the street was supposed to be answering it. Once again, new visitors to our house would become curious when a muffled phone began ringing and nobody made any effort to answer it.

Having this added phone line in the house did not come without opportunities to have a little fun with the system. Once, my sister was working at the car wash, and my father and I were sitting in the kitchen at home. The kitchen phone rang, Dad picked it up, and it was my sister's idiot boyfriend. Dad told the guy that Jenni was down the street at the car wash. Two seconds later, the phone in the closet rang, and this time I picked it up. Logically this guy assumed that I was at the car wash. He asked to talk to Jenni. I told him she wasn't there. He said,

"Well, I just called your house, and your dad says she's there."

I responded, "Well, I'm standing here in the car wash, and I can tell you, she is not here."

Two seconds later the phone rang in the kitchen. "I just talked to John, and he says that Jenni is not at the car wash."

Again, Dad told him Jenni was not at home either. At this point, the guy gave up.

Somehow news of our little fun eventually made it to Jenni. Boyfriend probably mentioned that she was hard to get a hold of, and she told him that she was sitting in the empty car wash all afternoon. Needless to say, she did not find the same humor in this bit that Dad and I did.

Anybody who has attempted to run their own business knows that it is *much* more restrictive than working for somebody else. For this reason, we never left town during the busy season of winter. If it was not for the sheer volume of customers we catered to during this time, it was also a form of risk mitigation. Dad lived with a healthy caution that the car wash's boiler may malfunction at any moment and the entire facility would turn into a giant ice cube over night. I can still picture my dad watching down the street from the living room on really cold nights for the stream of smoke spewing out of the boiler stack, intermittent confirmation that it was still running.

During summer, though, we would leave the neighborhood and visit the log cabin that my parents owned two hundred miles away on the northern edge of Wisconsin. Even as kids, we could tell that departing for extended periods of time really stressed my parents out. They had to get everything in order for the business to run on its own, with only a skeleton crew of attendants left behind. To raise tensions even higher, their cabin had no line of communication to the outside world. There was no telephone, and this was years before the advent of cell phones or email for the general population.

Mom and Dad's worst fears came to life one year when we had spent a week up in the north woods. This was during the time period I have termed "the first generation" of car wash attendants. They had been employees for years, so they had the routine down pat. The wildcard of panic was still at play though.

Let me back up for just one moment. I should explain at this point that, when first built, the car wash came equipped with a top-of-the-line alarm system with sensors on all doors leading into the building. The company that installed the security system told us that it would compete well with the systems that many banks at the time were using. I do not fully understand what was being protected with this security system; once the money was taken out of the building each night, there was not much to steal from the premises other than the car wash equipment itself. At that, Speedee Car Wash was less vulnerable than our competitors. Their facilities were open non-stop, and people could just walk in at any hour. Our business had this alarm system, and the attendant armed it by punching in a code on a keypad before locking the front door each night. If said attendant took too long to get out the door, the alarm sounded. And the alarm was ridiculously LOUD. Imagine a car alarm, but one hundred times louder. You could seriously hear the alarm from a mile away. The police were not notified, and no security personnel came running, but the whole neighborhood would be woken up.

So, back to our family vacation. While we were gone, the attendant one night was closing up when something went wrong in setting the alarm. Moments after closing the door, the alarm started to sound. To make matters worse, he could not get back in to disarm the system, because he had accidently locked his only set of keys in the building. This is when panic set in. Soon the police did show up, because somebody in the neighborhood called 911 to report that the building had been broken into. They arrived to find the panic-stricken attendant trying to find a way into the building. He had the idea that he could shimmy his way through the only window—the one in the back garage door. Realistic details like the fact that the window was at least five feet off the ground, and that it was only six inches tall did not creep into his decision-making process until he already broke the glass. He now had a broken window, and he was still outside looking in as the alarm blared. At some point during this whole debacle, Dad's friend Ken arrived on the scene with the spare set of car wash keys. In the end, the only real damage was a broken window and a terribly embarrassed car wash attendant. Needless to say, any relaxation that my parents achieved during vacation quickly evaporated upon coming home to that.

Another facet to being anchored to the business was the inability to "call in sick" to work. I often heard of classmates in high school or college staying out too late or just not feeling like going in to work, so they would feign illness. (OK, even as an adult, I still hear people doing this.) With a family-run business, that was not an option. First of all, Mom and Dad knew when we were really sick. But, more importantly, our replacements also lived in the same house, so they would not take kindly to that crap either. This left me with a work ethic that if I call in sick to work, you can be sure that I am near death.

There was one Sunday morning when Scott should have called in sick, but he knew the score and came to work come hell or high water. The night before had been one of those Saturday nights where he did not bother going home between shutting down the car wash Saturday night and opening it again Sunday morning. He had stayed out all night with his buddies drinking, so by the time his next shift was to begin, he was nursing a healthy hangover. Dad noticed something was up, because Scott parked his car at the car wash and began walking toward the house to pick up the keys like he did most mornings, but as he walked across our neighbor's lot, he had his head kind of tilted to the side, and he was vomiting as he walked. As he stood at the back door waiting for Dad to answer the door, he was throwing up off of the side of our back porch. That is the only time that I know of that Dad sent an employee home on account of being unfit for service. And then one of us got pulled out of bed and thrown into the game. *Surprise! You are working at the car wash today.*

Job Description

On the surface, working at the car wash was a pretty simple assignment. The basic principal was that, as attendants, we were there to assist the customers, prevent unruly customers from damaging the building or equipment, and perform some light maintenance. Under intended circumstances (note: I am careful not to use the term "normal"), patrons pulled their cars into one of the twelve wash bays. We would walk up to customers, greet them, and ask if they needed any change for the machine. In some instances, it was obvious that a customer had no idea how to work the equipment, so then we would offer a quick overview of how to do so.

Keep in mind, as far as self-service car washes go, ours was fairly simplistic compared to those of today. A customer would place $1.75 in quarters into the machine, and it would run for three minutes. While the machine was running, there was a red LED light on the front to indicate that it was on. There was a single dial selector that let customers control what was coming out of the spray nozzle. The options only included "Wash" (warm, soapy water), "Rinse" (warm, clear water), "Spray Wax" (warm spray-on car wax, and "Foamy Brush" (which caused thick, foaming soap to ooze out of a long-handled scrub brush.) There was a spot on the dial marked "Off," but in reality any of the six additional unmarked positions on the dial had the same effect as off, which caused all fluids to stop flowing to the stall but did not stop the three-minute countdown timer from proceeding (much to the dismay of many newbie customers who learned this nuance the hard way). This detail prompted exchanges like the following:

> Customer: "So, how do I stop the time?"
> Dad: "You can't stop time."
> Customer: "But I think you should make it so that I can stop the time."
> Dad: "Look . . . if you turn the switch to off, the hose will stop spraying, but the time will continue to count down."
> Customer: "But I think I should be able to stop time."
> Dad: "OK, fine! I'll make you a deal. If you can figure out how to stop time, you come back here, and I'll give you a thousand dollars."

Compared to the original Speedee Car Wash that my father first bought, this was cutting edge technology. I barely remember it myself, but the original car wash only presented customers a toggle switch with two choices: "Wash" and "Rinse." There were no indicators lit when the machine was running; customers had to use their own wits to figure out that when the pressurized water hose went limp and the spraying water ceased, time had expired. And in those days, there was no brush offered—foaming or otherwise.

But toward the latter half of the modern Speedee Car Wash's run, the technology started to show its age. Other car washes in the area emerged that sported fancier controllers with nearly double the number of options on the dial. Tire cleaner, spot-free rinse, prewash . . . these were all selections that we did not offer our customers. The machines themselves were getting more sophisticated too, not just the fluids they dispensed. Many had the feature of an audible beeping noise that indicated when time was running out, so customers could extend the time by inserting just another one or two quarters. Why buy another whole three minutes if an additional twenty-five seconds will do? Some of our competition even went so far as to have digital displays that showed a constant countdown clock. Those clever bastards!

Our machines had none of these bells and whistles, and most customers were sure to not let that point go unnoticed. One of the most common arguments with customers went like this:

Customer: "I couldn't hear the machine beeping, so I ran out of time."
Attendant: "Our machines don't beep."
Customer: "Well then, you should have a sign that says that your machines don't beep."
Attendant: "We cannot possibly put up signs that indicate everything our machines *don't* do. Because there is no sign stating that they *do* beep, you should assume that they *don't* beep."
Customer: "What do you mean?" (Looking confused.)
Attendant: "I mean, should we also put up a sign that the machine does not flash lights at you? Should we put up a sign that says it does not accept arcade tokens? Should we put up a sign that says the machine does not cook frozen burritos? There are all sorts of things our machines *don't* do."
Customer: "You're an asshole!"

(We all had this conversation so many times, we pretty much developed the customary company answers as presented above.)

Aside from the building and equipment, our personal standard issue gear for the job was simple. During the cooler half of the year, the uniform consisted of a navy-blue work jacket with "Speedee Car Wash—Thirteenth & Layton" embroidered in bright-yellow scripted letters across the back. Early on in the car wash's history, my parents got a few employees jackets with their names embroidered on the front left chest. But then it became evident that many attendants would be around little longer than some of the customers, so it was impractical to have personalized jackets for everyone. By the time I was officially on the payroll, all of the jackets were unassigned and hanging in the pump room on the side of the boiler. Most were the same size, but one was slightly smaller; that's the one my sister wore. Even with that one though, the sleeves were too long, and she always had to roll them up so that her hands actually stuck out of the ends.

As far as I know, everybody utilized the pockets on the jackets the same way. In the left pocket, we had a few handfuls of quarters. At the beginning of a shift, or upon replenishing our quarter supply, we could fit maybe thirty dollars in quarters in the pocket. In the right side pocket, we kept a folded stack of paper bills to make change with. Dad always encouraged us to keep as little cash on us as possible. Since we were not supposed to break anything above a twenty dollar bill, this required that we only carry a couple of tens, a few fives, and a handful of singles. Scott, for one, didn't take these warnings to heart. Never one to follow rules or shy away from danger, Scott loved to accumulate a huge wad of cash in his pocket. It was not unusual to watch Scott make change by pulling out a stack of bills easily totaling into the hundreds. It's a wonder none of us ever got mugged throughout our car wash days.

During warmer weather, the jackets were too warm, so they were set aside in lieu of canvas nail aprons. They still had two pockets, so the arrangement remained the same: quarters on the left, paper money on the right. But the money aprons did lack the official appearance that came with the embroidered jackets. If we approached first-time customers in our T-shirts, shorts, and money aprons, some of them did not initially comprehend that we worked there. I met a couple of rookie customers who misinterpreted my "Do you need any quarters?" for "Do you have any quarters?" and thinking that I was begging for money. I remember my parents toying with the idea of getting us uniform T-shirts for summers, but that never came to fruition.

We attendants prided ourselves on our change-making abilities. We did not have the luxury of digital cash registers like our peers working at McDonald's. We actually had to do math in our heads! And counting quarters quickly is a skill that we all developed out of sheer necessity. Most of us could judge the feel of up to ten dollars in quarters in our left hand to within fifty cents one way or the other. And the true mark of a professional quarter counter is the technique. An amateur will just willy-nillly grab a jumbled handful of quarters and pick them up four at a time from their other hand. A true pro though will get a nice roll of quarters preemptively aligned along the middle finger of his left hand and thumb through stacks of four with his right hand. So, take that, all of you critics who told us we could have been easily replaced by change machines with bad attitudes.

To fully understand life at the car wash, it helps to get a feel for the lay of the land. The car wash stalls were laid out like a small indoor parking lot with angled parking. There was a single drive-through door at the front of the building and a single drive-through door at the back of the building; all vehicles entered through the front door and exited through the rear door. The building had six bays on each side of the main driving aisle that ran down the center. Upon driving into the building, customers either turned to the left or the right in order to pull into their particular wash bay, which itself was a dead end.

If you put twelve angled spots into a rectangular building, you can imagine that there are two small triangular spaces at the front of the building in the corners. This is where two pump rooms housed the car wash equipment. The south pump room became home base for the attendants for two reasons: It had the building's boiler in it, so in winter it was much warmer than the north pump room, which did not have any substantial heat sources. And it housed the building's only telephone, so it was the sole connection to the outside world for a lonely attendant on a boring day.

As the primary hangout for idle car wash staff, the south pump room developed its own odd ambience and decor as time went on. A signature piece that hung in the room as far back as I can remember was a poster on the side of the boiler. Anybody who grew up in the Milwaukee area in the 1980s will remember the used car pitchman Crazy Jim and his infamous biannual events at the Hales Corner's Speedway named Crazy Jim's Demo Derby. For those unfamiliar with this guy, legend has it that he legally had his first name changed to "Crazy." Enough said. As one of his many promotional gimmicks, Crazy Jim distributed posters showing a man (himself) and a woman sitting at a lunch counter with a sign on it that read: "No Shirt, No Shoes, No Service." The perspective of the poster was from behind the two people. The woman followed the letter of the law—she had on a shirt and shoes, but she was naked from the waist down. Jim was looking below the counter with a jaw-dropping expression on his face. As though the poster itself was not low brow enough, one of the early car wash employees cut out a cartoony balloon of paper and wrote a message coming of out Jim's mouth that said, "I'll have the tuna sandwich." I thought that was hysterical even before I understood why it was funny. That poster and balloon comment still hang in the south pump room today, nearly thirty years later.

I have a similar memory of the south pump room from when the car wash first opened. One of the high school guys who was then an attendant had cut out a page of women modeling bras from a Sunday newspaper advertising insert. The smiling girls hung on the wall above the rack of water pumps. I remember asking my mom why there were underwear ads in the pump room, and she just said, "I guess the guys like looking at girls in their underwear."

My mother was known for answering awkward questions with obvious, matter-of-fact responses. Like one time when my sister and I were very young and watching "Three's Company." (This seems like an odd programming choice for elementary school kids, but I suppose children's programming was not then what it is now.) Jack Tripper and his friend Larry were making a big deal about having a rubber available. I asked Mom what a rubber was.

She said, "It's something a man wears on his penis so that he doesn't get sick."

I said, "Hmmm . . . OK. Should I wear a rubber so I don't get sick?"

Mom replied simply, "No, I think you'll be OK without one."

The north pump room was an entirely different animal; it was much more utilitarian. It held any cash that the business had on hand for the day and some inventory of random car wash equipment spares. But aside from that, it only contained seven car wash pumps (the extra pump being for the engine degreasing stall), the building's air compressor, and some soap and wax tanks. It was merely an overgrown janitor's closet.

The car wash was normally open from eight o'clock in the morning until nine o'clock at night. Sundays and holidays it closed a few hours earlier, at six p.m. That left a default work day of thirteen hours, so a typical shift was six and a half hours, split right down the middle at two thirty. But with school schedules, we had the freedom to come up with any bizarre schedule among ourselves that we could all agree to. If that resulted in me working ten hours per week spread over five different days, then so be it. Or, if I instead chose to work twenty hours per week during busy winter months all within the span of just Saturday and Sunday, that too was fine. In either case, it was handy that my commute to work was only a two minute walk.

A final aspect to understand the job was the environment in which it took place. I do not want to give the misimpression that I thought the conditions were terrible . . . I have seen many jobs with much less pleasant surroundings. At the same time though, the car wash environment that the stories of this book took place in was less than comfortable. Essentially it was an outside job. Yes, the car wash facility was technically indoors, but we only closed the doors completely on really cold days. Often if the temperatures were above freezing *inside* the building, then at least the front door would remain open to give people the hint that we were open for business. So, in the summer we sweated, and in the winter we froze. It was wetter inside the building during winter, so that only contributed to making it feel even colder. Pacing back and forth down the center aisle to tend to customers, we could not help but get hit constantly from overspray from the wash stalls.

On busy days, we walked non-stop for our entire shift, miles and miles without ever leaving the building, which tended to be dimly lit, at least compared to the outside on a sunny day. The equipment was loud, and there was no escaping the noise. The pump rooms were extremely loud, especially if there was any combination of six pumps, the boiler, and the air compressor running simultaneously in such a small, enclosed space. And then there was the exhaust. Always having the potential of twelve cars running inside a building left a lingering exhaust scent that would not dissipate until the slow, dead days of summer. Looking back, comparing my car wash days to my current cubicle-dwelling life, I'll opt for sitting on my ass in my cozy cubicle, hands down. Even with the relative lack of excitement of my work life now compared to my car wash days, at least I am warm and dry, and I don't have anybody yelling at me or trying to get me fired.

Admittedly though . . . reminiscing about the sights, the smells, the sounds, and the feelings of Speedee Car Wash . . . I almost tear up when recounting my glory days and would not mind grabbing a pocket full of quarters to serve a few more shifts.

Corporate Policies

What became one of my guiding principles when dealing with the general public was something that I learned very early on during my career at Speedee Car Wash. That concept was that if I wanted to get somebody to follow the rules, I had to have some means of enforcing those rules. Our customers were not open to diplomatic negotiations. Without a threat of consequence, most people were not going to play by the house rules merely out of the kindness of their hearts.

This lesson was taught to me within my first week officially on the payroll. The corner lot on the other side of the car wash's north property line had at one time been my father and grandfather's Texaco station. But after sitting vacant for many years, it became a shady used car lot with some generic name like South Side Auto Sales or the like. We always called it "Shifty's" because the guys who ran it were just that—shifty. They epitomized every used car stereotype in the book. Plaid suits, cigars, greasy comb-overs, the whole nine-yards. When we were kids, my parents so mistrusted these guys that my sister and I were forbidden to even cut across their car lot. If we wanted to go around the corner, we had to walk all the way around, no shortcuts.

Because of the car lot's proximity, would-be customers often parked in our driveway and walked next door. This was on one hand just annoying, but on the other hand, our north driveway was pretty narrow, so having a car parked there could make it difficult for our actual customers to get back out onto the street. One of my first days on duty, I saw a guy parking his car in our driveway for the obvious reason of walking over to Shifty's. I approached him as he was getting out of his car and told him he could not park there.

He defiantly said, "Oh yeah, why not?"

I explained that he was blocking our customers from getting out.

Showing obvious lack of concern for the inconvenience he was causing, he asked, "And what the hell are you gonna do if I don't move my car?"

I was totally unprepared for that question. And, consequently, I did not know how to reply. Even though I already sensed my own lack of leverage, all I mustered was "I'm just asking for you to please move your car."

Laughing, he replied, "Please!? Fuck you, kid." And he walked away.

From that moment on, I knew that any rule that was going to be enforced had to have a consequence already in hand. The next time I was asked, "What are you gonna do about it?" I was going to have a threat ready for every possible scenario. People always made the poor assumption that we car wash attendants were helpless and had to just let the customers walk all over us. We had a few advantages on our side though. Chief among them was experience. We had the same stupid arguments all the time, so it became second nature to foresee how situations were going to unfold. Our other ace in the hole was home field advantage. We knew the building inside and out, we had access to everything, and we knew how to use those tools to get our way.

If there was one cardinal rule at Speedee Car Wash, it was "No Buckets Allowed." At the end of each splash wall that separated the individual wash bays, there were steel pylons to prevent cars from impacting the concrete block walls. Down the length of the building, every other one of these metal barricades had "NO BUCKETS" stenciled on it in big letters. For those rare customers who bothered to read the signs on the front of the building or next to the machine in each stall, there were more notes about not using buckets there too.

The bucket issue represented the crux of two different perspectives regarding what our business was. Most of our customers believed that they were buying a product from us—primarily soap and water. From that point of view, employing a bucket to catch some of the water to reuse after time had run out on the machine was just common sense. They had invested in a product, and they wanted to use that product for as long as possible.

From our perspective though, we were in the business of providing a service. For each $1.75 in quarters dropped in the machine, an almost insignificant portion of that went to buying soap and water. Most of our operating expenses were in the form of mortgage payments, property taxes, electricity, natural gas, and staff payroll. As far as we were concerned, customers were buying time in our facility. If customers bought three minutes of time, filled up their buckets, screwed around for the better part of an hour, and then finally bought three more minutes at the end to rinse off . . . they were taking advantage of our heat, light, and facility for sixty-six minutes but only paying for six of them. Prohibiting bucket use was just a means of us not getting taken advantage of in this manner. This logic held true on any day of business but even more so if we had a line of cars down the street waiting to get in the building while some guy took up a stall without paying any money.

Bucket wars thus became one of the frontline battles.

Some bucket users were obvious in their ignorance of the rules. They just filled up their buckets at the end of the stall for the entire world to see. These customers were pretty understanding in most cases when they were told that their bucket was not allowed.

Bigger problems developed when people tried to be sneaky about filling up a bucket. For any would-be covert bucket users in the audience who are reading this, I will tell you right now, you can't do it. If you think you can fill a bucket using a high-pressure spray gun and not make the distinctive sound of a bucket being filled by a high-pressure spray gun, you are an idiot. I always loved how people kind of tucked their buckets in front of one of their car's wheels so that we could not see it while standing in the main aisle of the building. Yet, why else would a legitimate car washer be staying in one spot for so long with that strange sound emanating? Then there was the even more well thought out scheme of filling the bucket while it was *in* the car. True, this dulled the noise, but were the risks worth it? I for one don't want the unintended overspray from a self-serve car wash giving my car's interior an accidental washing. Not to mention the risk of dumping the whole bucket in my car. That to me is just not worth saving the $1.75.

Little did they know it, but bucket washers were some of the most vulnerable rule breakers we had. This is because, at best, the rule they were breaking found them in the middle of washing their cars. They might be able to *wash* a car with a bucket and a sponge, but they would be hard pressed to *rinse* a car using those same tools. One could thus infer that even the most obnoxious bucket washers had in their minds that they were going to use our facilities one more time to rinse off at the end. Dealing with a bucket washer who would just absolutely not abandon his bucket was pretty easy. Dad had the foresight of designing the building such that each stall was on its own circuit breaker. A customer didn't want to get rid of his bucket? Fine, I would just kill the power so that when he went to rinse his car, the machine was useless. We bid farewell to at least a few customers throughout the years who drove off full of soap suds from their buckets.

More often, bucket washing did not escalate to the point of disabling the equipment. Once a customer was caught with a bucket, then the negotiating began. If we were in good moods, we might let them dump the bucket on their car. If they had already pissed us off, we might make them dump it right in the sewer. If they refused, a quick fix was to just kick the bucket over. (As I said, being a bucket washer left a customer a bit vulnerable . . . it's hard to protect the prize.)

Legend has it that one old school car wash attendant once dumped a bucket *on* a customer. I do not know if that is reality or just an urban legend. Although, I do know this guy, and he may be just crazy enough to have done it. After all, he had been let go from his previous job as a school bus driver after a fight broke out on his bus and he took the stance that both parties were guilty, so he put an end to the fight by knocking the two fighters' heads together like Larry used to do to the other Stooges. With that on his record, maybe dumping a bucket of water on a complete stranger was not that big of a stretch.

The epitome of bucket washers were those who brought a bucket of soapy, hot water from home, either in the passenger compartment or in the trunk of their cars. Come on, really? How do you even justify that to yourself? Isn't that like walking into a restaurant with a full meal in hand and asking to eat at one of the tables? Even if you plan to have dessert there, I cannot imagine that shit flies.

In a close second to bucket washing was the rule infraction of towel drying. Under most conditions, we looked the other way if customers wanted to dry off their cars inside the building. If there was a line of cars waiting to get into the building however, then we politely asked the dryers to leave. Unlike bucket washers, a towel dryer, when asked, could immediately get out of the building and free up some space. On busy days, we had a special sign we posted outside the front door to give folks a heads up that they would not be able to towel off in the building. The vast majority of customers recognized the situation and obliged accordingly.

But, like always, there was a vocal minority of customers who wrongly assumed they held all of the cards in the drying battle and that we were helpless to combat against their behavior. Unlike bucket washers, as far as they were concerned, towel dryers were already done paying for our services, so there was nothing left that we could hold over their heads to prevent them from drying off. What escaped them though was the fact that it takes a long time to dry a car, whereas it only takes a brief moment to re-wet a car.

These encounters made for some entertaining exchanges. Because we only hassled dryers on very busy days, this also meant that we usually had arguments about drying when there was more than one attendant on duty. There is nothing like the power in numbers to embolden one's cause, not to mention the satisfaction of having an audience.

Scott's favored drying retribution was to simply let the "doorknobs" (he called all caustic customers "doorknobs") finish drying and then start making their way out the back door. Scott would position himself in one of the last two stalls. If the stall was open, he would reach in his pocket and drop $1.75 in the machine, then spray down the car as it drove by. I also saw him walk up to an occupied stall when a customer was actively washing his car, take the spray wand out of that customer's hand, drop $1.75 in his hand, and say, "The next one is on me." He then used the spray nozzle to soak down the dry car as it drove by. That latter approach had the added charm that it appeared the doorknob customer was accidently getting sprayed down by a fellow incompetent car washer.

Watching Scott do this was a joy just because he took

so much pleasure in it himself. You know in the movie *A Christmas Story* whenever the neighborhood bully, Scott Farkus, unleashed his torments on Ralphie or his friends, Farkus just cackled madly at his own antics? This was Scott spraying down a customer's car. He loved every minute of it. (Have I stumbled upon something universal here in the name Scott?) On those days, Scott was not working for the money; it was for the love of the game.

In addition to being disobedient to us and rude to fellow waiting customers, drying in the building on a busy day was next to impossible. Since we only asked dryers to leave on really busy days, it was inevitable that there were eleven other cars being washed while this person was trying to dry. Overspray from adjacent stalls was unavoidable and would undo any drying progress in seconds. Thermodynamics were not on the side of the dryers either. Even if everybody in the building were for some reason to stop spraying simultaneously, the humidity level already in the building prevented true drying. It's the same phenomenon as when you try to dry off a bathroom mirror after a steamy shower. Within seconds, the mirror will re-fog. They were fighting a battle they could not win on several fronts.

A subtle twist on the towel drying dilemma was when customers refused to leave the building after closing time, busy or not. This was a problem not unique to Speedee Car Wash. Anybody who has waited tables for a living knows the dread of seeing customers walk in the front door minutes before closing time. For folks who would just absolutely not leave the building after repeated requests, I found it handy to turn off all of the lights on them. (Kind of the opposite effect of a bar trying to clear out its patrons.) The building was not that brightly lit to begin with. Turning out the lights left it almost pitch black. Even diehard towel dryers exited the building once they could no longer see their car two feet in front of them.

A technique that worked against most rule violations

was black-listing. We did not have the benefit of sophisticated computer databases on our side, but we did keep a running paper tally in the south pump room of pain-in-the-ass customers. Sometimes the offending party stuck in our minds vividly enough that we just had to refer to the list for verification. Other customers had such unique vehicles that they easily stuck out of the crowd. Customers assumed that they had anonymity on their side. However, we encountered true major league assholes infrequently enough that we remembered most of them.

Having a black-listed customer encounter on a really busy day was the best. We might see them waiting in line and wave them in, but we would direct them all of the way through the building and out the back door before they realized what happened.

As they drove by the attendant near the back door, they would roll down the window and say, "Hey, what the hell is going on?"

And we would reply, "What, you think we forgot about last time?"

Then there were those customers who were motivated by cheapness more than anything else. These people were not trying to break a rule per se; they were just trying to not pay full price for our services. I am of course talking about the use of slugs or other quarter imposters.

I estimate that for roughly the first half of my time at the car wash, we did not take any active measures to prevent the use of slugs in our coin-operated machines. Every once in a while we found a Canadian quarter, a peso, or an arcade token in the day's quarters. But this happened so infrequently it always appeared to be an honest mistake or the case of a person needing to scrape up just one more quarter for the final wash cycle. It did occur frequently enough that through the years we accumulated a vast collection of quarter-sized coins from around the world.

In the middle of my Speedee tenure, we hit a wave of one or more individuals dumping large amounts of slugs into the machines. These were slugs in the purest sense . . . round steel disks that had the same diameter and thickness as a quarter but in no other way actually resembled real currency. They were just flat and black with smooth edges. Some days we found the equivalent of ten to twenty dollars worth of these useless coins in the change boxes at closing time. That raised a red flag, so we took action.

Most of the fake quarters were magnetic, whereas the official US quarter is not. Recognizing this, my father installed a small but strong magnet inside each control head, about an inch into the coin slot. This was close enough to the beginning of the mechanism to prevent the counterfeit coins from registering on the quarter counting circuit but far enough in to prevent the patron from removing said offending coin. A low-tech option like this probably would have been a bad solution had an attendant not always been on duty.

As varied as the fake coins were, so too were the manners in which caught customers reacted to being found out. The truly spineless jumped in their cars and sped off as soon as they realized that their funny money jammed up the machine. Others opted for a defense of ignorance. "Oh, I didn't realize that I just put seven arcade tokens in the machine."

Similarly, folks might try to blame the previous customer. That argument rarely held much water though, and the logic would fall apart quickly.

"If it was the previous customer, why did they leave without finishing their last cycle?" This was even shakier ground in the cases where I could open the coin vault and show them that they were the first customer to have used that stall thus far that day.

And then there were the overgrown children who reacted by beating the hell out of the machine with the spray wand. Classy, isn't it?

The simplest and most commonplace policies on occasion rubbed some idiot the wrong way, and they would just explode. One quiet Saturday morning, I had just opened the business for the day, and a thirty-something guy drove his penis-compensating pickup truck into the building. He got out of his truck and kind of stumbled toward me. He was drinking a bottle of orange juice, but he reeked of alcohol. Evidently Friday night partying was blending seamlessly into Saturday morning chores for this one. He told me that he wanted five dollars in quarters and handed me a one hundred dollar bill. Like most businesses, we typically did not accept any bills over twenty dollars. Not only was that our standard operating procedure, but since this guy was literally the *first* customer of the day, unless he wanted one hundred dollars in quarters, I probably did not have enough cash yet to break the hundred. When I told him just that, he FLIPPED OUT, telling me that if I did not do as he wanted, he would drive over me with his truck. When I refused again, he whipped his half-full bottle of orange juice at me. Being at rather close range, he scored a direct hit. I told him to get the hell out, and he said he would be back and promised that he would kill me upon his return. Luckily the drunk bastard never found his way back. Ahhh, the beginning of yet another peaceful Saturday at Speedee Car Wash.

Dad's biggest pet peeve was when customers pulled the front half of their cars into the building and stopped in the middle of the door. Folks tended either to jump out or stay within their cars and start asking questions at this point. In winter, this was the quickest way to watch all of the heat escape from the building. In summer, it was just an annoyance. I did not find the issue as problematic as Dad during the warm season, but if he was there, I made sure to wave everybody past me into a stall.

This usually left me in an awkward position, as I'd be caught between my father getting angry because a customer's car was sitting in the front door and the customer getting angry because they wanted me to answer a question.

With the noise of the car wash equipment, the car itself, the radio, and traffic noise, I usually could not hear a word the driver said, so I just waved them through. "Yeah, yeah, yeah . . . just pull in. I'll walk down and talk to you." It became like that episode of "Seinfeld" where Jerry unknowingly agrees to wear the infamous "puffy shirt" on national TV because he could not hear what he had been asked.

Far too many times I encountered one of these customers doing something they should not have been, and they would argue, "But you told me I could!"

In confusion, I would reply, "When did I tell you that?"

"I asked you on my way in if I could sand blast my car in here and you said, 'Yeah, yeah, yeah.'"

Aside from the hard and fast rules, each day we encountered policy decisions regarding situations that had not presented themselves yet before. This in itself was astounding, how even toward the end of my days there, customers always came up with new and interesting proposals that I had yet heard. Sometimes the judgment on these plays was clear. Other times it was more like "I'll let this person do this because I don't think it's a big deal, but hopefully they are quick and leave before Dad comes in to see what is going on."

"Can I use a wash pan? It's not really a bucket."

"No."

"Can I jack up my car to wash the underside?"

"No."

"Can you cash a traveler's check?"

"No." (Honestly, I didn't even know what a traveler's check was. Hell, even today, I have traveled out of the country countless times, and I still don't know what a traveler's check is.)

"Can I let my kids wash my car?"

"Yes."

"Can I hand wax my car in here?"

"No."

"Can I wax my car in the back parking lot?"

"Sure, I don't care."

"I brought a ladder to stand on to wash the top of my van. Can I use that?"

"Ummm . . . sure." (Man, I hope Dad's not on his way over!)

"Can I borrow a sponge?"

"No, I don't even *have* any sponges to let you borrow." (This was an easier argument to make if the customer had not approached me in the south pump room amid the BOXES FULL OF SPONGES that other customers had left behind.)

"My friend and I have two really small cars. Can we pull into one stall and wash them together?"

"Sure." (These girls were kind of cute.)

"Can I vacuum my dog?"

"Sure." (We had a regular customer who vacuumed his dog frequently. The dog didn't seem to mind. Although, as Gary Larson taught us, it's hard to read the emotions of a Golden Retriever.)

"Can I use your bathroom?"

"No."

That was a frequent question. The car wash technically did not have a bathroom. We employees had to go next door to use the bathroom at the garage. And we were doing the car washing public a favor by not subjecting them to the garage bathroom. While I worked there, Jenni would get so disgusted with the facilities that she cleaned it herself every now and then. I think it is a safe bet that in the thirteen or so years since she resigned, the garage bathroom probably has not been washed.

A variant of the bathroom question came once from a Harley rider and caught me off guard.

Harley Guy: "Can I use your bathroom?"

Me: "No."

Harley Guy: "Can I take a piss in your sewer then?"

Me: "Ummm . . . I'd prefer if you didn't?"

Harley Guy: "What will you do to me if I piss in the sewer?"

Me: "Probably nothing."

I heard the sound of tinkle hitting sewer before I even got all of the way out of the stall.

While we are on the topic of the garage bathroom, that brings up another interesting point. The garage building and the car wash building shared a common concrete block wall. When first built, the north garage wall was an exterior wall. It then became an interior wall when the car wash was built. Not foreseeing this future addition, the exhaust vent from the garage bathroom exited to the outside world through the north wall of the garage. That is, until that no longer was the outside world, at which point, the bathroom vented into the second stall on the south side of the car wash. Given just the right conditions, this was another possible means of motivating customers to leave the building.

In response to all of our antics, one would think that we regularly had customers retaliate against us. But, for the most part, that rarely happened. Surprisingly we had the good fortune that not a single car wash employee was ever the victim of violence motivated by either revenge or robbery. In hindsight, I find this unbelievable. On a couple of occasions, Dad received an irate phone call in the days following an incident with an unruly patron. The customer would plead his case and try to get us fired because of our bad attitudes. Then Dad would demonstrate to them what a bad attitude was all about. To my father's credit, he always stood up for his employees. This was the case too if a customer demanded to speak to "the owner" while we were on duty. Dad always took our side in front of the customers. He might tear us a new asshole after the customer left, but he never did this in front of the customers. I have had many managers since who could stand to learn this lesson.

For a while, the most common form of retaliation was via tagging. We would piss off the wrong wanna-be gangbanger at the car wash during the day, so they would come back and graffiti the outside of the building at night. Sometimes it was just a couple of tags. A few times it was every exterior wall of the building. Toward the end of the car wash's days, it became so common that we were buying random shades of grey paint from the local paint store in bulk. Walls of the building with the greatest visibility became patchworks of grey rectangles. But given the opportunity to repaint a wall or take a good old-fashion ass kicking, I would still opt to pick up a paintbrush.

By the way, are you curious about the backlash that would befall Shifty's customers who parked in our driveway? Like anything else, we developed our own special brand of enforcement for that rule too. Let's just say that it was amazing how many times we carelessly parked our snowplow in the north driveway, preventing a used car browser from moving his car. I guess there were just some things that we could not do anything about.

The Degreaser

If there was one thing I hated about the car wash (aside from many of the customers), it was the engine degreasing stall. This was the thirteenth stall, and many times it seemed like a horror movie that had come to life.

The very purpose of the degreasing stall was to allow customers to participate in activities that would not be allowed in the more conventional car wash stalls of the main building. Some customers sought us out because of this capability; others found themselves relegated to the stall after being kicked out of the main car wash.

If I make an explanatory analogy to the degreasing stall using almost any other business setting, it sounds like an absurd idea.

As a laundromat: "Your clothes are too dirty and greasy to wash in our washing machines. But I have this machine over here that I'll let you wash just about *anything* in."

As a restaurant: "I'm not going to let you eat *that* in this restaurant, you'll make a huge mess! But there is this table out alongside the building that you can eat at."

Or as a hotel: "Hey, you can't bring that hooker into my hotel! But I have this dirty little room around back that I'll let you use."

But as bizarre as it may sound in retrospect, the engine degreasing stall was just another slice of normalcy at Speedee Car Wash—a place where the abnormal became normal. In fact, "the degreaser," as we came to call it, was one of the biggest money makers at the place, especially during the slow summer months. We could make more money in the degreaser on a nice summer Saturday morning than the rest of the business made the entire week. This was well understood by my father, so he made us open up on Saturdays no matter how inclement the weather. During the week, even a light sprinkle was grounds for calling a rain day and not opening. But on a Saturday morning, we were open rain or shine . . . the cadre of rednecks coming to use the engine degreaser did not care if it was raining. Their piece of shit restoration project was greasy no matter the weather.

In principle, the engine degreasing stall was genius. Go into any self-serve car wash in the country, and I am sure you will find a sign somewhere that says "No washing of greasy objects." Most of these same establishments probably do not have any attendants on duty to enforce that rule, but the point is clear that if a person's sole intent is to wash down anything under the hood of his car, he is not welcome. By having a stall dedicated to such activity, we not only welcomed those who were being shunned at other car washes, but we were also catering to their needs. The engine degreasing stall was function over form. It looked bad, it smelled bad, and it was in an unheated portion of the building. (This final element also meant that the service was seasonal. We shut the stall down late fall once ice started forming on the floor.) But the water pressure at the wand was cranked up higher than the other twelve stalls. The soap was also in a more concentrated form to attack grease, not just road grime. Customers were warned against washing the painted surface of their cars in the degreaser because the exterior paint was less formidable against this combination of high pressure water and high soap concentration.

Like with any great idea though, give the customers an inch, and they will demand the proverbial mile. What started off as an area with slightly lax house rules was interpreted by many customers to be a lawless land. The layout of the building fed into this too. The degreaser was a separate building itself. Although it shared one wall with the main car wash, we had to go outside of the main building and walk around to the north side of it to access the degreaser. This meant that customers in the degreaser had less supervision than those in the car wash proper. The numbers were also in their favor. If I was trying to attend to twelve customers in the car wash on a busy day, I had a lot less time to babysit whatever illicit activity was going on out in the degreaser.

What were the official rules of the degreaser? ("Official" may be misleading here, since there was less signage in the degreaser than in the main car wash.) Some of the rules were pretty common sense, like "No pouring chemicals down the sewer." Others were a bit more nuanced, in the interest of protecting our own liability, such as "No jacking up vehicles." (Doesn't sliding under a wet vehicle on a wet floor-jack sitting on a greasy, wet floor just sound like a bad idea?) But aside from these common sense rules, the rule set boiled down to a case-by-case basis.

A lot of times, we employees and my father were at odds over the many grey area situations. I remember I once let a truck driver back his semi tractor into the degreaser so that he could wash the grease off of the fifth wheel. Apparently seeing a semi sticking out of the car wash raised a red flag with Dad, so he came over to see what was going on. When he asked if I knew what was being washed in the degreaser, and I said yes, he was *pissed*. Apparently customers could wash greasy objects in there, but not *too* greasy. He told me that it was going to make a huge mess. And I was thinking, *Take a look around, I don't know how you remember this place looking before this guy got here, but it wasn't very pristine according to my recollection.*

In order that I did not let this happen again, Dad made me scrub the grease off the walls AND lights after that one. My high school self loathed the injustice of this action since I was pretty sure much of the grease I was scrubbing had accumulated during the preceding ten years of operations . . . not from the previous customer alone. That did become the greatest motivator for us to enforce the rules though—we were the ones who would ultimately be cleaning up whatever mess was left behind. Our own personal rule book for the degreaser then became a question of how much of a mess did we want to clean up after the customer left. (On a side note here, the fifth wheel degreaser story recently came up in conversation between my father and me. I'm pretty sure that almost twenty years after the fact, he is *still* pissed about that one!)

Cleaning the degreaser was an ordeal for all car wash employees. One of the early memories that has stuck with me from growing up around the car wash was when my sister and I happened upon longtime employee John Haag scrubbing the engine degreaser floor one summer day. (Prior to my generation of car wash attendants, John was the longest serving employee. He got the job immediately when the business opened, as his father was the electrician who did the electrical work while the building was being constructed.) We always got this industrial-strength, grease-annihilating floor cleaner from the same chemical company that sold us the soap and wax used in the car wash. In the car wash's early days, the floor cleaner was a pale yellow powder that was sprinkled on a wet floor, scrubbed with a brush, and power washed off. Seeing John shaking the powder on the floor, we asked what it was, and he replied simply, "It's dry piss." (You gotta love a guy who is not opposed to cursing at little kids.) The name seemed fitting, so my sister and I continued to refer to that cleaner as "dry piss" when we were the ones scrubbing the floor years later (even though the soap was then more orange than yellow).

As though scrubbing the nasty, greasy floor was not enough fun to be had, that chore paled in comparison to dredging out the degreasing stall's sewer. The degreaser had a much larger sewer than all of the other stalls. Or perhaps more correctly, the other twelve stalls shared a single holding tank for sewage whereas the degreasing stall had its own. It was a concrete pit approximately three feet wide, six feet long, and four feet deep, with expanded steel grating that fit over the opening. The grating had the appearance more of an industrial catwalk than a normal storm sewer. Beneath the opening, there was a typical sewer design. The outlet was toward the top of the pit so that solids could collect in the bottom and not go out through the drain pipe. A trap was also incorporated, like any household sink, so that liquids lighter than water (i.e. petroleum-based vehicle fluids) floated on the top. Thus, heavier-than-water solids and chemicals sank to the bottom, lighter-than-water fluids floated to the top, and the water itself drained out at the mid-level. This design also meant that there was always a permanent puddle of dank, stagnant water that we could easily see just inches below the steel grating.

All twelve of the standard car wash stalls emptied into a large sewer basin of similar design just inside the front door to the main building. On an as-needed basis (once every couple of years or so), a waste management company would pump out the main sewer when the solid accumulation became too deep. However, because of the nature of what was going on out in the degreasing stall, its sewer naturally filled at a much faster rate. Instead of frequently calling in the professional sewer sucker just for the degreaser, my father devised a technique whereby one of us lucky attendants dug out the solid matter from the sewer basin by using snow shovels and dumping it into the dumpster that was emptied each week. I seem to recall my sister always being spared from this particular duty.

It is hard to say exactly which stage of the sewer cleaning project was least desirable. When we would start, the sewage would be pretty deep. We picked it up through a lot of water, so we did it from floor level, which required us to bend over and dig at a level much deeper than the concrete floor we were standing on. As we made progress removing the sludge, the level would become too low to attack from this angle, forcing the shovel-wielding attendant to crawl down into the sewer and scoop the sewage up and out of the pit.

Although I have had many jobs through my young life, I have never been a grave digger. But with this duty at the car wash, I think I have come close. The sewer was definitely the size of a shallow concrete-lined grave. And I have to imagine the sewer smelled much worse. It is funny how, no matter what goes into a drain or sewer, if given enough time and stagnant water, sewage all starts to smell the same. Unlike my grave digging comrades, I at least had the benefit of never having to fill my hole back in.

One of the few rules actually posted on a sign in the stall was regarding an "environmental impact fee." As though washing accumulated engine fluids from under the hood of a car was not ecologically offensive enough, most customers also chose to use some type of spray-on degreasing agent. This typically came in a tall aerosol can resembling a can of spray paint. At the time I worked at the car wash, degreasing agents from various brands came in at least four varieties: original, heavy duty, foaming, and environmentally friendly. The sides of the cans had endless warnings about how toxic this stuff was and how it should not be rinsed into a sewer. This did beg the question of exactly how one was to remove it from an engine after applying it, but perhaps that is why customers came to us.

We charged customers choosing to use a can of degreaser an environmental impact fee on a per can basis. This fee increased a few times during my tenure at the car wash, but it was roughly the cost of buying the can of degreaser to begin with. If customers opted to use the environmentally friendly variety, we waived the fee. We also conveniently sold the environmentally friendly cans of product at the car wash for those customers who wanted to avoid the fee.

The engine degreasing battles presented yet another one of those skills applicable to no other business or job in the world as we all developed the uncanny ability to identify not only the presence of but also the *variety* of engine degreasing agent sprayed onto an engine based on smell alone. This came in handy when devious customers applied the degreaser off site and then drove in and claimed that they did not have anything on the engine. Or they would have a single can of the environmentally friendly degreaser for show but then covertly spray on a half dozen cans of the heavy duty when we stepped out. But aided by our trained noses, we knew when we had to delve further. And in the lawless land of the engine degreasing stall, I was not opposed to opening car doors looking for cans of spent degreaser. A search warrant? Hey, we were not the police.

Customers were smart enough to know that a lot of their hijinks would not fly in the main car wash, so they would try to sneak it into the degreasing stall. I estimate that less than half of what went on out there could truly be classified as engine degreasing. Do you run a restaurant and need to clean out your deep fryers? Sneak them into the degreaser! Do you have a pickup truck bed full of oil? Try to sneak it into the degreaser! Do you want to spray paint your car but don't want the mess at home? The dumb kid at Speedee Car Wash probably won't notice if you repurpose the engine degreasing stall as a paint booth for a few minutes!

Even amid all of the unintended creative uses for the degreasing stall, those that the area was intended for tended to be a pain in the ass more often than not as well. If customers took the premise strictly at face value, I could understand that if their engine blew out a head gasket and spewed oil all over the engine compartment, they would want to come over and clean up the mess after they repaired it. But most of the time, the "cars" being brought into the degreaser were well beyond that scenario. These were shade tree mechanic meets Frankenstein home project cars. Most had so much grease and oil visible under the hood, one could not really make out where the engine may actually be, if indeed it had one.

A bigger problem was that most of these hoopties barely made it onto the property under their own power. It did not take a genius to figure out that a car sputtering in on what sounded like its last breath was not going to fare well with having its electric ignition system power washed. I cannot recount how many jalopies I had to push out of the degreaser. It just became a normal part of the job—like signing our time cards. But the customers were always completely *shocked* that their dream machines would not restart. This outcome had never occurred to them, and most were unprepared to do anything about it when it did happen.

Luckily the lay of the parking lot was in our favor for getting stalled vehicles out of the building. To get into the degreaser, cars had to drive up a gradual hill leading to the door, such that the floor of the degreaser was about a foot or eighteen inches above the grade of the parking lot. Although this proved difficult for some of the struggling victims on their way in, it meant that we only had to push the stranded car out the door, and usually gravity did the rest.

The back door was also about eighteen inches above the surrounding parking lot level, but it did not have an asphalt ramp leading up to it. Because of this, the back garage door was permanently closed. So not only did vehicles need to be able to move under their own power to successfully navigate the degreaser stall, but they had to be able to move in *both* directions.

We all became pretty proficient at pushing around stalled vehicles. I learned early on that on the flat paved floor, I could push most cars by myself. Trucks were sometimes a little bit more difficult but still manageable.

The worst was when customers wanted to "help."

One such occurrence happened when my sister and I were both on shift. Since we were both working, and the degreaser was open for business, this must have been a Saturday or Sunday after a late spring snowfall. We were both tending to customers in the main car wash when we realized that the customer in a truck in the degreaser had been there for quite a while but had stopped feeding quarters into the machine. Jenni went out to talk to the guy, who told her that his truck would not start. Since it was a larger, heavier truck, she came back to recruit me. We told the guy to get into the driver's seat; he should steer and work the brakes while we pushed him onto the driveway. This came with the usual instruction of "Don't stop in the middle of the driveway!" (That only traded one problem for another.)

This plan started to unfold just as we described to the truck's owner, like it had many times before with other stranded vehicles. Jenni and I began pushing on the front end of the truck, and it started to slowly back out of the stall. Just then, the unexpected happened. The guy perceived that we were struggling too much, so he decided to get out and help. In an instant, he opened the door, jumped out, and had one hand on the steering wheel while he pulled on the truck's door to help. Jenni and I both immediately start yelling, "Get back in the truck! Get back in!"

If you can visualize the scene in your head, you can see what is about to happen. If not, go out into your own garage, open your driver's side door, and try to back out through the garage door. Unfortunately this individual did not have the benefit of such a mental exercise prior to making his decision to assist us.

In a mere matter of seconds, the relative silence was broken with the quiet yet distinctive crunching sound of a truck door being opened farther than its hinges were designed to allow. This sound though was cushioned from what it could have been, because you will recall that the truck's owner was helping us move the vehicle by pulling on the door. Now his arm was pinned between the truck's door and the inside rail of the garage door. The arm sandwich with two slices of door bread was strong enough that it completely absorbed the momentum of the rolling truck. Unbelievably, the man did not scream or even let out a peep. My sister and I instinctively ran to the other side of the truck and began pushing it back uphill into the degreaser. (Strangely, *this* time the driver opted to not help us, although now is really when we needed it.) Through some strange combination of physics and good luck, this guy seemingly did not suffer any major injuries, and the truck door was still able to close. He got back in the driver's seat; we told him to keep his ass in there this time; and we pushed him out onto the driveway as originally planned.

It was only ten or fifteen minutes later when the stranded driver reemerged. (He had nowhere to go, his truck still was not running.) He requested to speak to our manager. By this time, Dad had already been briefed on the latest bonehead we had encountered. So one of us went to get Dad again, and in typical fashion, the conversation went like this:

Dad: "Hi . . . you asked to talk to the owner?"
Customer: "Yeah, those kids made me push my truck out of the degreaser there, and the door of the truck got caught on the garage door. Now my truck's door is all bent up, and my arm kind of hurts." (To this day, my sister and I can still mimic the sad little motion he made

with his arm while he said this.)
Dad: "So why the hell didn't you stay in your truck like they told you? Those two can push a truck."

Apparently the customer could see that he was not going to get very far with that endeavor, as that was the last we ever heard from him.

In a similarly notable customer experience, I was a mere bystander. On this quiet Sunday summer afternoon, Dad and I had the day off, so Scott was manning the wash himself. Dad and I were watching something on television at home in our living room. Because of the placement of our house down the block in relation to the car wash, for better or worse, we could plainly see the front of the car wash while sitting comfortably in our living room. The degreaser was tucked back a little behind the front of the main car wash, so we could not see that with as much clarity, but we saw enough to grasp in general what was going on.

Dad must have just randomly glanced down the street, at which time he noticed smoke billowing out of the engine degreasing stall. He got up from his recliner, calmly walked to the other side of the living room, and placed a phone call down the street. We could hear the phone ring in the closet a couple of times, and then Scott picked up. When talking with my father, we could always tell when we were missing something very obvious, because in his signature sarcasm, he would start talking really slow, drawing out all of his words and referring to us by name incessantly. So the conversation that followed went:

Dad: "Heeeeey, Scooooooottttttt . . . what's going on in the engine degreaserrrrr?"
Scott: "I don't know, Uncle John. Why?"
Dad: "Scooooooottttttt . . . why is there smoooooooke coming out of the degreaser?"

Scott: "Hmmm . . . I don't know."
Dad: "Scooooooottttttt . . . why don't you hang up the phone and go check it out."

From our vantage point, we could see Scott slowly walk out of the main car wash and disappear behind the north wall to the degreaser. Dad always said that Scott would not move quickly for anything, even if the building was on fire, and oddly, we watched this proverb play out in reality. Scott was only out of our line of sight for a minute or less when he reemerged and slowly walked back into the car wash. A few seconds later, the house phone rang.

Dad: "Helloooo, Scooooooottttttt"
Scott: "Uncle John! The guy's car is on FIRE!"
Dad: "Scooooooottttttt . . . did you call the fire department or grab the fire extinguisher out of the garage?"
Scott: "No, I called you . . . you said you wanted to know what was going on."
Dad: "Weeellll . . . why don't you hang up the phone and do both of those things."

We then saw Scott meander over to the garage and reappear with the fire extinguisher. He must have called the fire department too, because they almost beat him to the degreaser. (It was advantageous that the fire department was kitty-corner from us.) The fire was quickly put out, and the car was evidently a big enough piece of crap to begin with that no real damage was done. Similarly, the building did not suffer any noticeable effects.

Other engine degreaser events were less climatic but none-the-less remarkable. One early morning, I was working by myself, and there was a guy washing his motorcycle in the degreaser. This by itself was rather unusual. Milwaukee, being home of Harley Davidson, never has a shortage of motorcycles driving the streets. We attracted our fair share of riders, since they did not have the option of going to full-service or drive-thru style tunnel car washes that only catered to enclosed vehicles. During big reunion events, which happen every five years, we got a lot of bikes. Most motorcyclists, Harley owners chief among them, are meticulous about keeping their motorcycles clean. We rarely made the bikers use the degreasing stall because most of the highly chromed motorcycle engines we saw were cleaner than most of the painted surfaces of the cars that drove through the front door. But if memory serves correctly, this was a less-cared-for specimen, a smaller Honda or Yamaha model, not a fancy "cruiser" or "crotch rocket" . . . it was just the standard run-of-the-mill street bike. The cleanliness of this motorcycle's engine relegated him out to the degreaser, and like many patrons before him, a good cleaning was all it took to immobilize the machine.

Unlike many of this man's four-wheeled counterparts, he was able to push his water-logged ride back out of the degreaser himself. I was not prepared, though, for the following request. After he tried all of the normal tricks to dry out the electric ignition system, he decided that he could manually start the engine by getting the bike up to speed and then dropping it into gear. What would provide the initial momentum to get the motorcycle and rider up to speed? Why, your friendly neighborhood car wash attendant of course! I do not remember if the man offered me my pick of being the pusher or the pushee, but since I had never driven a motorcycle, I was probably only qualified for one of the roles anyway. (Prior to this morning, I had not had any motorcycle *pushing* experience either, but obviously that skill can be picked up while on the job.)

So there we were, running up and down the north side of the car wash—me pushing this guy and his bike as fast as I could run, and then him trying to force the engine to start by dropping it into first gear. This was apparently something this guy had never done before either, because he took many tries . . . all unsuccessful. The bike usually popped a few times, lunged a couple of times, and then came to an unceremoniously abrupt stop, but it never did start. Did I mention that the design of this particular motorcycle was such that the only thing I could push was the shoulders of the driver himself? As if the scenario was not homoerotic enough to begin with, this certainly was the icing on that cake.

In hindsight, I bet that guy didn't have any engine problems after all.

Amid all of the bad experiences that came with manning the degreasing stall, I can think of at least one day where it was pretty cool to have the only such venue in town. Milwaukee is home to the aptly named Milwaukee Mile—one of the oldest auto racing tracks in the country. For well over a hundred years, the big names of motorsports have raced on this track, at different times hosting Indy Cars, stockcars, sports car racing, etc. During my tenure at the car wash, the Milwaukee Mile was hosting an annual NASCAR weekend. Although the major league NASCAR series (then the Winston Cup Series) did not come to the track in those days, the track did host a Supertruck race and a Busch Series race (the minor league of NASCAR in those days).

It was the day after the Busch race, and I was working at the car wash when a semi rolled onto the parking lot. Semis usually spelled trouble, but not this one. It was the car hauler for the DeWalt Busch series NASCAR. I let the guys pull the truck in the north driveway and park it right along the building. Businesses pay big money for appearances like this, but we were getting it for free. They rolled the car that had been competing out at The Mile just the day before into the degreaser. Dad told me that the standard rules did not apply to these guys. He said if they wanted to put their car up on jacks, they probably carried enough insurance to buy the whole place. Before I knew it, they had the entire car hoisted up, all of the wheels off, and the body panels coming off too.

The DeWalt crew dumped a lot of quarters into the degreaser that day. And we got some extra attention from people who noticed the race trailer but probably had never noticed the car wash prior to their visit. In the end, the guys left me with the obligatory picture of the driver and his car, which still hangs in the south pump room to this day. And to top it all off, they were one of the few customers who were not only able to restart their car after washing, but they did not leave a mess either. An occasional good day could happen even at Speedee Car Wash.

Professional Development

Winter met the car wash staff with cold weather, damp working conditions, and non-stop lines of cars coming through the front door. The colder it got outside, the more customers were drawn to Speedee because we were the *only* car wash in the city that was indoors and heated. During the three or four months of peak winter weather every season, we worked long, hard hours walking hundreds of miles inside the building and rarely getting a break from the cold, the wet, the noise, or the exhaust. Our hands would become numb from the cold. Gloves were not an option since we could not effectively count quarters with gloves on. And we often had to shovel snow inside the building because so many snow-covered vehicles came in just to blow the snow off. The building may have technically been "heated," but it was by no means warm and cozy. Temperatures were usually kept just high enough to keep the floor from turning into an ice-skating rink. The only relief was when we could spare a few moments to put our hands on one of the warm water circulation lines in the south pump room to temporarily regain the sense of touch. We definitely earned our minimum wages during winter.

On the other hand, summer months presented us with a completely different set of challenges. Long, grueling hours of hard work were replaced with endless hours of boredom. For the same reasons we were a popular destination in winter, we became irrelevant during the nice Milwaukee summers. "Indoor" and "heated" were not selling points in mid-July or August. Every self-serve car wash was heated at that point. And our indoor environment—a bright, welcome relief on a cold, dreary January day—was shadowy and confining in the midst of summer. Besides, most customers who sought out the self-service aspect in the name of economy viewed the option of washing their cars in their home driveways with the garden hose a much cheaper and preferred alternative during summer.

With no exaggeration, we could easily have as many cars during the first twenty minutes of a winter day as we may have through an entire day of business during summer. I remember opening the car wash many winter Saturdays and immediately filling up all twelve wash bays. And I would still have another half dozen waiting outside the door after that. In contrast, I also remember days in summer where I had less than ten cars all day long, from eight a.m. to nine p.m.

To my father's credit, he was very accommodating with his employees dealing with the boredom during the summer. I think he felt that it was payback for the "combat duty" (as he always called it) that we served during winter. Between the non-stop work during winter, and the complete lack of work during summer, it all kind of evened out.

The default entertainment options to battle the boredom were basically reading or listening to the radio. At the risk of sounding like an old man here, this was in the days before laptops, Wi-Fi, iPods, smart phones and the many other portable diversion devices that most of us carry now at all times. In my high school and college days, I was not an avid reader, certainly not reading for recreation. So in that regard, the car wash's imposed reading time was good for me. It forced me to visit the library often, and I grew an appreciation for non-fiction that I carry to this day. But, not being naturally drawn to books, I could only read for two to three hours per shift before I got antsy and had to move on to something else. Likewise, I could listen to music for a couple of hours, but that too became mundane. On a six- or eight-hour summer shift, that still left at least a couple of hours to kill.

The irony here is that I always attended academically demanding schools. This resulted in me having a lot of homework to do during the winter months when the car wash was usually too busy to allow me to do my studies on the job, while in summer, I had plenty of study time, but school was not in session.

I am not sure which idiom is more appropriate here: "Necessity is the mother of invention" or "Idle hands are the devil's playground." Both could describe a car wash attendant left to his own devices to fill countless hours of boredom each week.

I think that one of the more common pastimes on the job flowed naturally from one of our assigned duties. I will be direct and call it what it was: We were garbage pickers. Scattered in and around the building were at least six to eight steel drums that had been repurposed as trash cans for customers' use. Part of our job was to roll a dumpster around the building and unload the individual cans into the dumpster that the trash men would pick up. Most of the trash was what one would expect to find when cleaning out a car—fast food packaging, empty soda bottles, used napkins / tissues, and newspapers. But amid all of the normal refuse, an interesting specimen could not help but catch our eyes every now and then.

Somewhere along the way, the car wash had acquired a litter picking tool. Essentially it was a wooden handle with a metal point at the end. Sometimes you see park workers wandering around with these things making litter kabobs and scraping the litter off into a trash can. I imagine that one of us had found the tool itself in the trash, and thereafter it was used to poke through the other trash.

There was a bit of an art to garbage picking. I learned early on when digging for treasure, DO NOT open tied plastic bags. If somebody has gone to the trouble of double knotting a plastic grocery bag that they have thrown away . . . it is probably for good reason.

One sought-after trash commodity at the time was the

empty packaging from Marlboro cigarettes. During those years, each pack of smokes came with a proof of purchase that had a small barcode and an assigned number of "Marlboro Miles." Much like the Kool-Aid points on the back of Kool-Aid packets, people could collect various amounts of miles to redeem for Marlboro branded merchandise. None of us being smokers, we would nominate one employee to run across the street to the Clark station to grab a redemption book, and we collected Marlboro Miles all summer long to see how many we could accumulate by the redemption period's deadline. The south pump room held a box full of miles, so when the time came, we counted and divvyed them up, each selecting what we wanted from the catalog of premiums. Considering none of us smoked, we had an impressive selection of Marlboro merchandise. T-shirts, sweatshirts, hats, blankets, lighters, flashlights, a stopwatch, a lantern, a radio . . . if they were giving it away, we probably had at least one of them. (You may be wondering why we opted to get a cigarette lighter if none of us smoked. Well, there was a little bit of a pyro in each of us! Throwing flaming paper airplanes, lighting firecrackers, and melting plastic utensils were just a few of our lighter fueled pastimes.) And to think, we had gotten all of this stuff for free, just because we were willing to dig through the trash a bit. It was amazing how much our Marlboro smoking customers were just giving away.

Another often-found commodity in the trash was porn. Being raised in an admittedly sheltered childhood, this was as much an education as any other experience at the car wash. And given the caliber of some of our customers, I do mean *education.* For example, prior to stumbling upon it once in the dumpster, I was naive enough in my young life to not know that there was a publication named *BLT— Buns, Legs, & Tits.* The name really said it all. Based on the one issue I saw, there was no claiming that anyone was buying this magazine for the articles. Unless one counts single lines of text scrawled across nude collages such as "Wall to wall the way you like it!" as legitimate reading. There was also an issue of *Chicks with Dicks* in the dumpster one time. They say there are some images that you cannot unsee, and this periodical was one of those cases. I am not sure if these were Photoshopped images or actual photographs of shemales, but I think I sleep better at night then and now not knowing. That mystery is just another plastic bag in life that I am not going to untie.

One of the best things I ever found in the garbage was an RCA brand digital walkman with graphic equalizer and reversible cassette deck. At the time, a device like that was retailing for one to two hundred dollars. I have no idea why somebody threw it out, but I pulled it out of the trash, put in a crappy cassette (discovered on a previous dumpster diving expedition), and found that it still worked. In fact, it worked so well, I *still* have that damn thing today! The most ironic part is that while working at the car wash, I saved up some of my hard-earned cash to buy a high-end dual cassette deck for my home stereo that I spent hundreds of dollars on. Through the test of time, that unit no longer works, but the one I found in the trash is going strong. (Maybe my frustration in college was not the only allure to a career in refuse services.)

One of the worst things I ever found in the trash was dirty diapers. I would just be poking through the dumpster with the old garbage poker and then *WHAM!* . . . there it was . . . poopy diaper. It caught me by surprise every time. Looking back, this perplexes me. As a parent myself now, I have changed my fair share of dirty diapers. The number of times my wife and I had no choice but to change a diaper in one of our vehicles could probably be counted on one hand. Within that subset of occurrences, the number of times I just threw the dirty diaper in the center counsel with the empty soda cans and fast food trash was ZERO! Who is driving around with dirty diapers in their cars until they go to the car wash to clean house?

Wait, I take that back. The *worst* thing to find in the trash was butchered deer carcasses. We could count on this occurring at least once or twice during each firearm deer season in Wisconsin. Apparently the hunters took out the edible portions and left the rest in the bed of their pickups to dispose of in our back lot. There is no sensation that can match the surprise of peering into a trash can expecting to see fast food wrappers and paper bags and instead finding hooves and entrails. Aside from the gruesome discovery, this also presented a problem with heft too. The unwanted parts of a deer are pretty heavy when all stuffed into one trash can. We had to be able to pick the trash can up off the ground at least four feet and flip it upside down to empty it into the rolling dumpster. All deer parts combined on occasion prevented this feat, requiring one to manually pull the parts out of the can piece by piece. I do not remember hearing about this portion of the job during my recruitment! The only saving grace here was that by hunting season it was usually cold enough that the pieces were at least in a partially frozen state.

Like with any other skill, one had to learn to garbage pick with some finesse. It was uncouth to just dig down in there when customers were around. I usually waited until early in the morning or late in the evening when the place was completely empty. Once, my sister made the unfortunate choice of digging through the dumpster after it had been rolled out into the front parking lot awaiting the weekly garbage truck visit. A car load of guys drove by hanging out the window and chanting, "Digging in the traa-aaash!!!" She was horrified.

A closely related offshoot to garbage picking was sifting through the crap that people sucked into the vacuums. This required a higher level of boredom and a lowering of expectations. The vacuums only had to be emptied maybe once every couple of weeks. Most of the time, its contents looked a lot like the contents of a home vacuum cleaner bag.

Lots of dust, dirt, hair, pebbles, etc. There was always a lot of broken glass too. I guess if you smash a car window, the car wash is your logical first destination. Unfortunately it was not uncommon to find vomit in there as well. (I will point out that the first sight of vomit spelled "game over" for me.) There was an inordinate number of car cigarette lighters sucked in to the vacuums because most folks underestimated their strength. (Do you remember when cars came with cigarette lighters as a standard feature?) But what we were really after was change. People either knowingly or unknowingly sucked up handfuls of change from their cars. It might take an hour or two to sift through all of the useless debris in the vacuum bin, but we might come away with ten to twenty dollars in coins. Considering we were only making on the order of five to six dollars an hour, it was a well-paying endeavor.

We did not have to go out of our way to find all of our distractions from the constant boredom during the summer months. Some entertainment opportunities landed right in our laps. One of the most popular among car wash staffers was fielding phone calls for Leo's Pizza. (For reasons that are about to become obvious to you, "Leo's Pizza" is a fictitious name made up for the purpose of retelling this story.) Speedee Car Wash had the blessing / curse of having a phone number that was only one digit off from a local pizza delivery shop— one had a two where the other had a four. On a standard touchtone phone, I do not think that accidently pushing the two instead of the four is an easy mistake, or even the most obvious mistake for that matter, but it certainly happened a lot. (For a while, we suspected that a phone book got printed with a typo in it, but the calls continued for decades, long after any single misprint would have gone obsolete.) This phenomenon became the ultimate prank phone call . . . the victim being the one initiating the prank.

There were various forms of fun we could have when receiving a Leo's Pizza phone call. In its most basic form, the exchange went like this:

Phone rings.
Car Wash Attendant: "Good afternoon. Speedee Car Wash."
Caller: "Is this Leo's Pizza?"
Car Wash Attendant: "No."
Click . . . Caller hangs up.

Ten seconds later . . . phone rings again.
Car Wash Attendant: "This still isn't Leo's Pizza."
Caller: "Fuck you!"
Click . . . Caller hangs up.

*Ten seconds later . . . phone rings **again.***
Car Wash Attendant: "Good Afternoon. **Leo's Pizza!**"
Caller: "Hi! I'd like to place an order for delivery . . ."
Car Wash attendant then proceeds to take the order, "calculate" a total, and promise that the pizza will be delivered in thirty minutes or less. (I think the thirty minutes or less deal was actually a Dominos offer, but it was obvious at this point that we were not dealing with a real detail-oriented individual.)

Let's examine this situation just a bit. First of all, we have already established that the caller could not dial a phone in the first place. And we politely informed them of this during the first call. But what made the caller think that pushing the redial button was going to connect the call to someplace different the second time around? Or the third? The calls always came in such rapid succession that the caller had to be hitting redial, not simply punching in the same wrong number multiple times.

This also demonstrates how little people listen to each other. It was always amazing to answer the phone clearly stating "Speedee Car Wash" and then being asked,

"Is this Leo's Pizza?" And, by the third call, shouldn't some recognition have set in that the voice was the same as the one from the first two conversations?

As I said, the above scenario was the game in its purest form. We had a lot of time on our hands though, and a lot of Leo's Pizza callers, so we were able to improve upon the basic theme. One of my favorites was to answer the call the second time already masquerading as Leo's Pizza. (Honestly, on Friday or Saturday nights, you could answer the first time as Leo's Pizza. Who calls a car wash at seven p.m. on a Saturday night?) At this point, I would take on the role of the worst Leo's Pizza employee who ever lived:

Me: "Good evening. Leo's Pizza."
Caller: "Hi, I'd like to order a pizza to be delivered."
Me: "Sure, no problem, what would you like?"
Caller: "I want a large pizza with pepperoni and sausage."
Me: "OK, one medium vegetarian pizza."
Caller: "What? No, I said a large pizza. With pepperoni and sausage."
Me: "Oh, I'm sorry. A small pizza with just cheese on it."

The game continued until the caller got completely frustrated and hung up. In lieu of feigning incompetence, other good fun was to see how ridiculous of a situation we could contrive and get the pizza customer to still believe. For example, "I'm sorry, our oven is malfunctioning tonight. Would it be OK if the driver delivered your food to you uncooked? You have an oven, don't you?" Or, after the caller told us his address, it was fun to see if we could convince him that he did not live that far away, so he should just walk over and get the food himself. After all, our drivers were *very* busy; they could not be tied up with all of these short trips down the block.

A rare delight was when I took a call, promised delivery in thirty minutes, and then the pizza buyer actually called back at about the forty-minute mark demanding to know where their pizza was. Any of the above acts could be adapted here. Confusion, incompetence, personal attacks . . . the prank had already played out by this point, anything beyond here was just frosting on the cake.

Do I feel bad for any of the Leo's Pizza high jinks? Not really. In my mind, we were doing Leo's Pizza a favor. These clowns could not even dial the phone correctly. I am sure they would not have been able to pay or known their correct address, or they would have communicated their order wrong. As for the callers, in most cases they had two opportunities to figure out that something was going wrong. Three strikes, you're out . . . learn how to dial a damn phone.

I watched Scott put a new spin on this game too by taking on the role of the pizza caller when he was not on duty at the car wash. Dad and I were in the living room, and Jenni was working at the car wash. From the house phone, Scott called down the street to the car wash, donning his best Middle Eastern accent. ("Best" really is on a relative scale here. Scott was by no measures a skilled impressionist. All of his imitated voices basically sounded like this one, so we were not often fooled.)

Scott: "Hello! Pizza-pizza!"
Jenni: "Pizza pizza? That's Little Caesar's. Isn't this Leo's Pizza?"

Like usual, Scott was laughing too much at his own shtick by this point to carry on any further.

Also of note in this regard was a less common yet no less entertaining occurrence that happened on the other side of the car wash's south wall. When the Olive Garden chain first hit Milwaukee, it was a pretty big deal. (As though Milwaukeeans had never partook of Italian food before.) Being the days before the Internet when would-be restaurant patrons wanted to call the restaurant prior to the yellow pages being updated for the year, they would call directory assistance. Seemingly the folks who worked at directory assistance may have also been some of our Leo's Pizza callers. From their perspective "Olive Garden" . . . "Oliva's Garage" . . . close enough! The most memorable Olive Garden call my father received unfolded like this:

Dad: "Good morning. Oliva's Garage."
Caller: "Hi, I'd like to make a reservation."
Dad: "Oooookaaaayyy . . . I usually call them appointments, but whatever. . . . What kind of car do you have?"
Caller: "Why do you care what kind of car I have? I just want a table for four."
Dad: "A table? I don't have a single table in this place. I suppose I could put some boards across one of the floor hoists."
Caller: "What are you talking about? Is this the Olive Garden???"
Dad: "Noooo . . . it's not the Olive Garden. Let's try starting this conversation from the beginning." *Pause.* "Good morning. OLIVA'S GARAGE."
Silence . . . Click

Amid all of the Leo's Pizza and Olive Garden calls, I'm not sure we ever got a single phone call actually intended for Speedee Car Wash.

Boredom really became fun when there was more than one car wash attendant on site. In winter, business was heavy enough that it was not unusual to double up on shifts. In summer though, it was never the case that two attendants were actually needed at once. It was more the circumstance that, at shift change, the employee coming on duty may show up thirty minutes or an hour early, and the person finishing up their day might similarly stay beyond their quitting time. At the official shift change time, the money apron and keys would be handed over unceremoniously just in case a customer accidentally showed up to wash a car. I'm not sure if you should classify this phenomenon as some sort of compassionate camaraderie, trying to support each other in our boredom, or as a sad evaluation of the inactive social lives we led away from the car wash.

In a minor act of divine intervention, the movie *Clerks* hit theaters during my stint at the car wash and brought along with it an answer to our boredom. This classic Jay and Silent Bob movie chronicled the antics of two convenience store clerks. Disgruntled, bored, and dealing with the general public in a mindless job, they portrayed a lifestyle that the staff of Speedee Car Wash already knew all too well. In the movie, the characters pass time by playing street hockey on the roof of the store while on shift. Inspired by this stroke of genius, we also took up street hockey inside the car wash. At first, our attempts were improvised and rather ghetto. Early games took place using two broom handles for sticks, and for a puck we alternatively used either an abandoned gas cap or a crushed aluminum can. As time went on, and car wash hockey proved to be more than the typical passing diversion, we actually started to invest in better equipment. We bought some legitimate street hockey sticks and one of those pucks that has balls trapped in it so that it rolls across the floor nicely. On a couple of occasions, we went so far as trying to play on skates, but that was difficult on the wet floor and awkward if a customer actually showed up. Arguing with customers was painful enough without the disadvantage of being the freak on roller skates for the encounter. We did speculate though that if we were to go so far as donning full pads, the advantage would once again be on our side. When we did away with the skates, we opted instead to reduce floor friction by spraying them all down with water before a game. The speed bumps at each end of the building served as our makeshift goals. We looked into buying real street hockey goals, but those were prohibitively expensive. It was bad enough that we were already spending money to help alleviate boredom at work. Even at the time, it seemed counterintuitive to spend money to have fun while at work, which had the original intent of making money.

With two of us on site, there were all sorts of other games more pathetic than hockey to pass the time. For example, a book of matches discovered in the trash may lead to a game of "I bet I can hold on to a lit match longer than you can." Or how about the always-entertaining game of "Let's roll an old tennis ball out into the intersection and see what happens"?

All generations of car wash employees seemed to dabble in fireworks. There was just something about lighting off M-80s and cherry bombs in an enclosed building to really make a hell of a bang. Dropping lit bottle rockets into the sewers was fun too, because if we directed them just right, we could get them to run down the length of the building, releasing a small puff of smoke through each stall's sewer as it went. We heard growing up that some of our attendant predecessors repurposed a handle from one of the car wash foaming brushes to be used as a bazooka-style bottle rocket launcher. In this manner, one attendant aimed the unit and held it over his shoulder, while the other lit the fuse from behind. Scott and I found that although this was visually appealing, we also needed to incorporate something on the end of the tube to provide a bit of back pressure for the rocket to begin its liftoff. The gas cap that had also been used as a hockey puck on occasion served this purpose nicely.

Since there was never a short supply of quarters or other coins, those too became play things for us. We all became proficient at the useless skill of balancing a stack of quarters on our elbows and then quickly reaching around with the hand of that same arm and trying to catch the quarters before they fell. We were easily into the five or ten dollar range on that measure. (I can wait if you want to go give it a try yourself.) We were less successful at the game of "Drop a handful of change on the floor and I'll tell you how much it was just by the sound." But we competed nevertheless.

Dad discovered a design element of the car wash ceiling after all of his employees already had. The steel roof of the building had foam insulation to trap a bit of the heat inside during winter. This foam was just the right density and stiffness that if we propelled a quarter perpendicularly to the roof, it would get lodged in the insulation. Dad found this out when doing some repair work near the ceiling by the south pump room; he happened upon handfuls of quarters hanging from the roof. Those quarters are all still there; Dad says it is his retirement fund.

Perhaps the most legendary use of free time while on shift comes from two of the earliest employees: John Haag and Jim Sterle. John and Jim, like us later, spent a lot of time at the car wash, both when they were on the payroll and not. Dad walked into the car wash one hot summer afternoon expecting to find John, but he instead found Jim. When Dad asked where John was, Jim motioned to the south pump room. Dad cautiously walked into the room to find John stripped down to his underwear and up to his chin in the five-hundred-gallon water supply tank. This water, having come indirectly from the depths of Lake Michigan, typically hovered in the forty to fifty degree range, even in the peak summer months.

Jim said, "I bet him twenty bucks that he couldn't stay in there for fifteen minutes. You got five more minutes to go, buddy!"

Think about that the next time you are at your friendly neighborhood car wash. There is a small yet finite possibility that the crystal clear water you are washing your car with just served as a cold bath for a very bored employee trying to pass some time and make a few extra dollars. And try not to act too surprised if you find an employee bent over with his head in a trash can either.

Clientele

Please allow me to address those starry-eyed young men and women out there who bought this book in the hopes that they could glean from these pages all of my secrets to breaking into the self-service car wash business. Sadly, the only advice I can share on that matter is to be born into it. Like John-John Kennedy or Hank Williams, Jr., winning the genetic lottery is the only way I know to get this gig.

And while we are on the topic of crushing dreams, let me also offer this unsolicited advice to rising stars in the car wash biz: If you are expecting to see a lot of girls in bikinis getting all sudsed up while washing their sports cars, let me just warn you up front that it will likely happen less frequently than you have been led to believe.

I think the first time I encountered this Hollywood-perpetrated car wash myth was in the movie *Cool Hand Luke*. In some class I took during high school, this movie was misconstrued as educational, so we watched it during class in lieu of a week's worth of normal lectures. It may have been an American literature class, or perhaps theology . . . I really do not remember. Hell, I don't even remember what the movie was about. Prison? Paul Newman? That's about the extent of what I took away from it. That is, except for the infamous car wash scene! That has been burned into my memory for eternity.

For those who have not seen the movie: Toward the beginning of the film, there is a scene where some of the prison inmates are working in a chain gang performing manual labor out in the community. Seemingly to torment the prisoners, a beautiful woman in the neighborhood decides to wash her car, and we'll just say that she *really* gets into it. Go check it out on YouTube if you have never seen this. It's worth the effort.

Now, mind you, I attended an all-male Catholic high school. This was in the days before the Church's problems with sexual abuse fully came to light, so our teachers were probably a bit more liberal than they would be today. The teacher presenting *Cool Hand Luke* rewound the tape and let us watch the car wash scene at least two or three times. Looking back, the great irony in this is that while we were sitting there ogling this woman, most of us were actually less likely to have contact with a real female than any of the incarcerated men in the movie.

I can rattle off a bunch of similar scenes throughout the years in pop culture. Jessica Simpson paid homage to her *Cool Hand Luke* predecessor in her video for "These Boots Are Made for Walkin'" from the *Dukes of Hazard* movie soundtrack. There were similar scenes in *Wild Things, Bring it On, Bad Teacher*, and countless others. And how could we overlook the entire movie franchise dedicated to the genre—*The Bikini Car Wash Company* and *The Bikini Car Wash Company II*? Cinematic masterpieces that all Americans can be proud to have shared with the world.

For all of these instances, I am sure it is easy to fall under the impression that working at the car wash during summer months must have been a better deal than working at a water park that only let sorority girls in. But unless Speedee Car Wash was the exception rather than the norm (which it very well may have been), I speak from experience when I say that it just doesn't happen.

The closest that this fantasy ever came to reality at Speedee Car Wash actually occurred down the street and around the corner. (That still counts, right?) During my years at Speedee, there was a young woman who lived in one of the apartment complexes in the neighborhood. She owned a mid-1960s Corvette Stingray—canary yellow. On at least two occasions, I happened to be driving through the neighborhood at just the right time to see her washing her car in a matching canary-yellow string bikini. She was not as engrossed in her work as her *Cool Hand Luke* mentor, but kudos to her for making the effort. Besides, any woman who makes wardrobe decisions based on her vehicle is doing good in my book, even more so if we are talking swimwear.

On the other hand, the closest this scenario ever *really* played out *within* the walls of Speedee Car Wash was even a bit further from the spirit of the scene. We had a repeat customer who visited during the winter months. She drove a little Suzuki Sidekick mini-SUV. And despite the cool temperatures, she also opted to wash her vehicle while wearing shorts and a string bikini top. The critical element of this development though was that this woman was much more generously proportioned than the general public normally deems acceptable to be wearing a bikini in the first place. Fashion critics will tell you that choosing a flattering outfit is all about accentuating your best features and redirecting attention from those you are not so proud of. In this regard, maybe this girl would not have been so obvious if her swimsuit was not so small or, for that matter, if her vehicle was not so small. These both combined to make her look larger than life. Not to mention it was freezing out, which only made her stand out even more. But I must give her credit for having the self-confidence to put it all out there. You go, girl.

While on the topic of customers who stick in my memory due to unusual behaviors, there was a cross-dressing man who drove a white step-side pickup truck, and given the fact that this guy was out doing the chore of washing his truck, he did not dress as I would expect a cross-dresser to dress. This was not a full-on drag queen heading out for a night of clubbing. This was more him going out to do laundry and grocery shopping. So on the scorecard of cross-dressing, his attempt was kind of half-assed. The outfit consisted of jeans, a sweatshirt, ladies pumps, some feminine jewelry (necklace, bracelet), and a really bad curly, long wig. Actually, this person closely resembled a teacher in my high school at the time. However, the teacher had the misfortune that his crappy-looking hair was natural, not a wig.

And then there was the weirdo we all termed "Wide Guy." As one may expect, Wide Guy earned his nickname based solely on physical appearances. He had a very unusual physique in that he was kind of short and stocky, but from chest to back, he was not really that thick. We always mused that from the front, he looked like a fat guy, but if he turned so that we were looking at his side, he disappeared. Like a two-dimensional cartoon character that is only the thickness of the paper it is drawn upon.

Wide Guy had some other bizarre tendencies that made him stand out from the crowd. He typically came to the car wash wearing Green Bay Packers sweatpants and a matching sweatshirt. This was not unusual in Wisconsin, where they will banish you from the state if you do not pledge your allegiance to The Pack. But he always paired the sweat suit with fuzzy bedroom slippers, a less than ideal choice of footwear in a wet car wash.

Then there were his cars. Wide Guy drove crap. Again, not remarkable in itself. We had a lot of customers who washed cars that many would reason had higher priority needs than washing. (If your car cannot restart after washing its exterior, maybe the car wash should not be your first stop.) What made Wide Guy stand out is that he took such pride in washing his jalopies. Not only that, but he frequently painted them as well. And for many reasons, chief among them lack of skill and proper equipment, he should not have been painting his own cars. Sometimes he painted the car elsewhere, presumably at home. I remember asking him one time, "Wasn't your car blue the last time you were here?" He announced with pride that he had painted it only days earlier. (You could see the brush strokes in the paint.) On a couple of other occasions, he used cans of spray paint to paint his car in the back parking lot of our car wash. He washed and dried like any other day, fired up a dozen or so cans of paint, and left with a different colored piece of crap than he drove in with. Look out, Maaco! Consumers have an alternative that can undercut even your prices!

Thrown into the menagerie that we called our customer base, there were also a handful of legitimately nice people who visited frequently, followed the rules, and were pleasant to deal with. Some kind of kept to themselves, so we never got to know them. For example, there was a white Jeep Grand Cherokee driven by a young woman who I believe lived one block away on Fourteenth Street. She had a personalized license plate that said, "INTENSE," and for that reason, that is all we ever knew her as. She came in wearing a medical uniform once or twice, so we fell under the impression that she was a paramedic or worked in an emergency room or the like. (Maybe "INTENSE" was a play on "intensive care"?) But the point is that Intense came in just about every week throughout the whole year. She never requested to do any crazy stuff, and she probably spent around five dollars during each visit. Dad always said that if we had just a few hundred more customers like her, operating the business would not have been such a chore.

Another unnamed regular customer was a guy who drove an enormous pickup truck that was fully outfitted to do combat against Wisconsin's snow and ice. Based strictly on appearances and wardrobe, I always got the idea that this guy was ex-military. He usually wore combat fatigues and tall black paratrooper boots, so I referred to him as "GI Joe." He had a fully hydraulic Western blade hanging on the front of his truck, a salt spreading hopper taking up the entire bed, and a hard-to-miss light bar on the cab. He could almost give the municipal plows in Milwaukee a run for their money. Undoubtedly, this vehicle represented a huge investment, and as such, he was willing to spend some money to keep it in good shape. It was not unusual for him to come in after major snow storms and ask for thirty dollars in quarters right off the bat. Oh, sure, he was a seasonal customer, but when dropping that amount of money per visit, we were happy to have him be one.

And chief among all customers was Ron Jenkins. Ron was the epitome of a regular customer. Ron Jenkins was to Speedee Carwash what Norm Peterson was to "Cheers." Just like the "Cheers" theme song says, if you are a good customer at any establishment, it becomes a place where "everybody knows your name." This was Ron. If you are an *exceptional* customer, you will know it, because you get invited to social gatherings with the business's staff after hours. This too was Ron. He and his wife, Dianne, attended my sister's college graduation party and a few other non-car-wash events.

Ron had a lively background and the accompanying inexhaustible supply of stories that made him fit right in. He had done a stint playing college football and was drafted to play in the NFL. He joined the Oakland Raiders before completing his college education. Like so many stories told by Bryant Gumbel, even though Ron had grown up poor, he quickly adapted to living the good life of a pro athlete. But within his first or second season, he suffered a career-ending injury. He went from living the good life to being unemployed with no marketable skills. He was able to bounce back though, and when he started frequenting the car wash, he and his wife were leading a typical middle-class existence on the south side of Milwaukee just a few blocks from the car wash.

When I initially met Ron, he was a truck driver hauling shipping containers off of freight trains to locations throughout the Milwaukee area. He later got a job at a foundry where he was still primarily a truck driver but also got tasked with other odds and ends around the business. We told Ron stories of the car wash, and he always had stories to share either from his current life or from back in his football days. In my opinion, some of his best material came from the foundry job. The place was run by an old redneck white guy who had a penchant for hiring illegal Mexican immigrants to man the foundry. Most of the Mexicans did not speak English. And because Ron was black, the boss assumed he could speak Spanish. (This seems like an obvious conclusion, right?) Ron thus became the unofficial translator at the company, even though he spoke no Spanish. The boss said things like, "Hey, Ron, go tell all of those guys over there to stop fucking around."

Ron would turn around and say to them, "Hey, guys, the boss says that you gotta stop fuckin' around." One would think that with enough linguistic demonstrations like this to prove his translation skills, the requests would stop, but they did not.

Throughout my tenure at the car wash, Ron was a twice-a-week customer, usually making at least one visit on the weekend. First he would wash his pickup truck, and then he came back with his wife's vehicle. Sometimes he brought one in on Saturday and the other on Sunday. Ron easily spent one to two hours washing each vehicle. We never minded in the least. Ron always brought great conversation, and talking to him for an hour or so was certainly better than the normal mundane crawl of mornings at the car wash. The only way we knew that Ron had stayed longer than he should was when Dianne would call and ask, "Is Ron still there washing his truck? Can you send him home now?"

So, Ron . . . Intense . . . GI Joe . . . if you are reading this, know that you were some of the few bright spots at the car wash, and it did not go unnoticed. We always enjoyed having you visit and wished we had more customers like you. Hell, I'm sure if you stopped by, Dad may let you in to have another wash even today.

Wide Guy, on the other hand . . . Super Wash is on Twenty-Seventh and College. I don't know what their painting policy is though.

Market Research

Companies devote an awful lot of effort toward trying to figure out their customers' opinions regarding the products and services that said company is offering. Telemarketers, online surveys, comment cards, guys in airport terminals chasing people down with clipboards . . . it appears that market research has become as ubiquitous as advertising. Companies seem to put as much effort into luring customers in to buy their goods as they do asking "How did you hear about us?" At Speedee Car Wash, we never took any measures to find out what our customers were thinking. (My dad would be quick to point out that based on experimental evidence, our customers were not doing too much thinking at all.) However, we never suffered from a lack of customer opinion data either. Most people driving through the front door were all too willing to share their thoughts with us, whether we wanted to hear them or not. And it was rarely anything positive.

A lot of the complaints we received somehow involved time. We sold our car washing service in increments of time, so time was a paramount topic. Perhaps the laws have been updated since I left the state of Wisconsin, but when I worked at the car wash, the bureau of weights and measures made a distinction regarding coin-operated time-based machines with a line in the sand drawn at the one dollar charge. If a service cost less than a dollar, then a company was not required to display on the machine the duration the purchase was netting the buyer. For machines costing more than a dollar, the time period had to be shown on the machine and had to be accurate to within plus or minus two percent.

As such, the vacuums in front of the building were fifty cents and seventy-five cents (depending on which strength vacuum you chose) for four minutes, but because they were less than a dollar, the four-minute time span was not shown anywhere on the machine. Inside the building, the car wash machines were $1.75 for three minutes, with "3 Minutes" prominently displayed right beside the price. Because the vacuums did not have a time posted, most customers never thought twice before, during, or after their purchase about how long the machine ran. The "3 Minutes" note on the car wash machines in the building though was just an invitation to scrutiny. A lot of people instinctively assumed that the stated time was a hoax and we were out to screw them.

The most typical way for this complaint to unfold was that customers dropped their quarters into a machine and washed for three minutes, likely with the intention of washing their vehicles in just one cycle. When they could not achieve that feat (as most people could not), they naturally assumed that the machine had only run for maybe a single minute . . . maybe two minutes tops. So then they would come and complain to us, saying they wanted their money back. Our standard approach to this confrontation was to not refund their money. However, if they would buy a second round, we would time that cycle and refund any money they had been mischarged. Since three minutes equates to one hundred and eighty seconds, the pricing was convenient in that the time structure was exactly one cent per second of washing.

Acting as judge and jury for this challenge was our official Marlboro brand stopwatch. Prior to acquiring this device, we had used a run-of-the-mill digital stopwatch for these timing exercises. But the paranoid few who thought the machines were inappropriately timed also assumed that we obtained a trick stopwatch that reported a false three minute reading to coincide with the false timing on the machines. It's funny how Marlboro branding lent credibility to the proceedings. Oh sure, those bastards at Speedee Car

Wash may have been able to find some generic stopwatch that runs too fast, but how would they get a Marlboro stopwatch that also did so.

From my point of view, this was a rigged match from the onset. Dad meticulously timed each control head and fine tuned the timing circuit so that each ran a second or two longer than three minutes. (Inside the machine, there was a tiny potentiometer that adjusted the timing to any length of time.) Experience showed that the timing remained very consistent. So I would stand next to the customers as they dropped their seven quarters into the box. While they were doing this, I would hold up the stopwatch so that they could see both that it started at zero and that I did not hit start until the final quarter dropped in the machine and the water pressure came on. The customers then began frantically running around their cars washing and rinsing. They were already spending double what they had intended to spend, so they certainly were not taking any chances on having to do a *third* round. From their perspective, the three minutes flashed by in an instant. From my perspective, time stood still, and I could see clearly each millisecond tick by on the watch. As the three minutes of agony approached its conclusion, I would approach the customer, displaying the stopwatch to them, and click it off as the water pressure cut off.

"There you go, three minutes and three seconds. You were right, the timing is a bit off, and we *under*charged you. Between the first cycle and the second cycle, you owe me six cents." I do not think anybody ever paid me for the discrepancy. If they did, I am sure it was in the form of throwing pennies at me.

Another time-based complaint that sometimes had more validity was that when switching from the high pressure wash setting to the high pressure rinse, the machine did not transition over quickly enough. That is, people complained that the rinse water continued to have soap in it. There were several physical phenomenon working against us on this issue. (Warning! I am about to nerd out on you here. If technical details tend to make your eyes glaze over and your mind to wander, feel free to skip ahead to the next paragraph.) The actual switching took place in the pump rooms where a solenoid was triggered to allow or prevent the soap solution from entering the water stream. Both the soapy water and the clear rinse water traveled down the same line from the pump room to the pressure wand in the customer's hand. Consequently, the fluid needed time to get down the line, but when switching from wash to rinse, the residual soap also had to be cleaned off of the walls of the line, which further prolonged the transition. If a customer was in the stall right next to the pump room, let's say that the conversion could happen in as little as five seconds—not too bad in my opinion. But the last stall at Speedee was six times as far from the pump room as the first one. This left six times as far for the clear water to travel and six times as much line to rinse out along the way. The palatable five seconds turned into at least thirty seconds . . . nearly twenty percent of the three minutes bought in the first place. Savvy customers could plan ahead for this lag time, but it understandably caught many patrons by surprise.

All of those legitimate concerns led some customers to see soap where there was none to see. Our rinse water was pretty warm. Warm water is rarely clear. (Go pour yourself a glass of hot water from your kitchen sink and tell me how clear it looks.) This cloudy water was falsely accused of being soapy water. Pressurized water itself is also not crystal clear in appearance. When the water stream coming from the spray wand impinged on the smooth surface of a vehicle, it was a very turbulent flow regime that prompted the formation of millions of tiny air bubbles on the surface. These bubbles too were misidentified as soap.

And, finally, customers often used a spot on the floor as a litmus test of whether there was still soap in the water or not. But the floor almost always had soap on it. Thus it was just as likely they were creating soap bubbles from preexisting soap on the floor as it was that there was still soap in the water coming out of the wand. Unfortunately the complaints became so persistent that our solution was to dial back the soap concentration in the wash cycle. Less soap in the wash water left less to clear out when it switched to rinse. For all of the complaints we received about soapy rinse water, I do not remember anybody complaining about lack of soap in the wash water.

A fun complaint to deal with was "Hey, your vacuums suck!"

The canned response was "Well, thank you very much."

The customer who had just been caught off guard by a twist of his own words would reply, "No, I mean your vacuums *don't* suck."

And I might reply, "Thank you again?"

Any complaint regarding the vacuums lack of sucking power typically translated into "I'm a dumbass and I just sucked my T-shirt into the vacuum, so now the hose is clogged up." The vacuums, especially the higher priced seventy-five cent ones, had a sucking power that would make most home shop-vacs blush out of inadequacy. Wait . . . let me restate that. The vacuums, especially the higher priced seventy-five cent ones, had a sucking power that would make most female porn stars blush out of inadequacy. People accidently vacuumed things into them all of the time that they did not think the machines had the power to nab—car keys, cigarette lighters, wedding rings, etc. Instead of owning up to their mistakes, customers would rather just submit the complaint that our equipment was to blame.

When it was time for one of us attendants to unclog a vacuum hose, we had about as low-tech of a solution as we could possibly muster. Our default vacuum fixing tool was a long length of one-inch diameter water pipe that was perhaps ten feet long. We would simply jam the pipe in the end of the hose and start mashing down on the blockage, giving the appearance of a Civil War soldier brushing out the barrel of field artillery between rounds. Even if the clog was farther into the hose than the length of the pipe, we could still get a hold of the pipe by kinking the loose end of the hose around the pipe's end. Like plunging a toilet, usually we hit a sweet spot on the obstruction, knocked it loose, and let the vacuum take over, leaving the line quickly cleared out. Never getting to see the blockage because of this rendered any incriminating evidence to the customer as lost.

Things got more involved if the blockage was *in* the vacuum itself. This first required that I unlock and remove the bin that caught all of the vacuumed debris. With this out of the way, I had to stick my arm up into the machine to feel around for whatever was choking off the flow. It was always advisable to wait until the vacuum was shut off before doing this maneuver, which required a deep reach up into the unseen inner workings of the vacuum, well past my elbow . . . halfway to my shoulder. It was usually an easy task at this point to grab the offending object with my hand and pull it out. My arm though would be completely grey, coated in dust, cigarette ashes, and hair. It was like I had artificially inseminated a cow that had not seen any action in a *really* long time.

Even the lowly disposable towels that we sold to customers interested in drying their cars after washing were not immune from being caught in the sites of the complaining masses. We had two towel dispensing vending machines in the car wash. The premium "Blue Shams" were sold in a stainless steel machine toward the front of the building. It was mounted on the wall near where the attendant typically sat. These were some cross between fabric and paper, and as the name implied, they were blue in color. (I believe the "sham" portion of the name was supposed to conjure the epitome of vehicle drying, a natural animal hide chamois. Not a "sham" as in the fraud or con that many customers concluded.) A Blue Sham sold for a whopping fifty cents. The sales pitches on the side of the towel machine instigated some of the complaints against the towels. Claims of "durable" and "reusable" may have been overstated. We reused them all of the time, so technically that part was correct. But if they got dirty, they didn't really lend themselves to being laundered. Another claim on the vending machine was "bath size." I don't know how crappy the bathroom facilities are in the homes of the Blue Sham marketers, but I think by most standards the Blue Shams were little larger than hand towels.

Given the shaky marketing claims on the towel machine, it came as no surprise that some customers were not happy with their purchase when it fell to the bottom of the machine. With the look of disappointment on their faces, you would swear these people were expecting a Martha Stewart designed full-size terry cloth bath towel to come out neatly folded and tied with a delicate ribbon. Come on . . . what do you expect for fifty cents?

The mechanics of the machine also caused some issues. It worked under simple principles: Drop two quarters in the coin slot, pull the pinball-like knob, and the towel drops to the bottom of the machine, similar to a candy bar being dispensed from a vending machine. But the mechanically disadvantaged had trouble with every step of this process. Some people jammed the coins in so fast that they fell straight through the machine. (I think this was intended functionality on the part of the machine designer to weed out overweight counterfeit coins.) Others managed to squeeze the coins in at an angle, getting them stuck between the internal coin slot and the machine's external housing. Still for others, once the coins were successfully in, the simple mechanical command of "Pull" above the knob evaded some. These customers would push or turn or shake side-to-side. And for those who managed to get all of the way to the towel falling to the bottom of the machine, many still could not figure out where the towel went, as though they were expecting the machine's entire front end to open like an old-fashioned newspaper machine.

All of the mechanical issues with the towel machine did leave us attendants looking like wizards in this regard. If customers got stuck at any point through the towel purchasing process, they would either come find us, or we would hear them beating the hell out of the machine. It helped that we were usually sitting only a few feet away. Once we were called in to assist, we could work the machine effortlessly. It was like Fonzie controlling the diner's jukebox with a well-placed hit. (Yes, being a Milwaukee native, I am required to make at least one "Happy Days" or "Laverne & Shirley" reference. But contrary to the often-asked questions since I have left Milwaukee, no, I did not actually know any of the characters when growing up.)

Another element of the Blue Sham legacy that prompted whining was when our supplier decided to stop individually packaging each towel. Initially each fifty-cent towel came wrapped in a flimsy cellophane wrapper. Of course, these wrappers were inevitably cast aside in haste and found blowing around the building and parking lot. So it was no big loss to us when the towels started being shipped without the wrappers. Customers immediately assumed the worst. "Those bastards at Speedee Car Wash have found yet another way to save a couple of pennies!" They assumed we had forgone the wrappers as a cheaper alternative but were still charging the same fifty cents. (As if we could switch the machine over to dispensing the cheaper towels for forty-nine cents owing to the penny that we saved on packaging.) More practical customers complained that the towels were now becoming damp while in the machine. Without their plastic wrapper to fend off the humid environment, it was proposed that the towels no longer had the same drying capacity as when they came wrapped. When voiced to management, I believe my father relayed the message through us. "Tell them they can jam the towels up their asses." For the truly budget-conscious consumer, there was a low-cost alternative to the Blue Sham. For a mere twenty-five cents (half the cost!), customers could walk to the far end of the building and buy a "Giant Towel" from a yellow vending machine bolted to the east wall. The Giant Towels were a lot more paper-towel-like than their Blue Sham cousins. These were just white folded paper towels, not much larger than one would find in public restrooms. On the ranking of every measure—quality, durability, absorption—I would pay the additional quarter and go for the Blue Sham.

These are just a few examples of the most often heard complaints. There too were the endless little nit-picky complaints about the business, the equipment, and how things were run. Any possible facet of the operation was open to constant public scrutiny: We should be open earlier. We should stay open later. The prices are too high. The building is not warm enough. The building is not bright enough. The attendants have bad attitudes. The attendants do not look presentable. The attendants should not be allowed to read while on the job. And on and on and on . . . Finally there were a couple of complaints that happened maybe only once, but they entertained us staff, and thus became part of the oral history of the business. A guy complained to my father once, "The pressure coming out of the water gun is terrible! I can piss harder than this thing!"

My dad replied, "Oh yeah? I bet you can't do it for three minutes though."

And on the opposite end of the spectrum, I once had a customer in the degreaser indirectly complain that the pressure was *too* high. I'm not sure what he was expecting, but as soon as his accomplice started the machine by dropping in the last quarter, I heard screams of "Make it stop! Make it stop!"

Based on all of the above, I left the car wash believing that most people can find something to bitch about for any possible topic. Conventional wisdom states that in a system that only has two allowable outcomes, you are bound to disappoint half of the people no matter which result occurs. I think that is way too optimistic. If a group of people predicted the outcome of a coin toss, one group would be disappointed that the result was not heads, another that it was not tails. But another group would whine that the wrong type of coin was used or that the tossing conditions were inappropriate or propose that the toss was all a conspiracy and a trick coin was used because the World Bank had decided the outcome of the toss last week.

If you do not believe this trait of human nature, go to any online news outlet and, at random, choose a news article. No matter how mundane the content of the article, the comments section that follows will have idiots bitching endlessly about every conceivable take on the news. I recently saw a short article that was merely a statement of fact that as last year came to a close, market research indicated that airline prices had risen some stated percentage from the year previous. To me, this was just a simple conveyance of information. To the whining public, it was another solicitation for their opinion. The comments included things on the order of:

"The airlines are to blame! They are all money hungry machines that don't care at all about their customers!"

"The air traveling public is to blame! As long as you idiots keep paying the higher ticket prices, the airlines have no motivation to stop raising prices! Boycott air travel today!"

"Delta Air Lines lost my bag!" (There is an obligatory comment for each article that is almost entirely unrelated to the news at hand.)

Alas, if after reading the commentaries you still do not believe that people can complain about anything—and I do mean *anything*—I invite you to go work at a self-serve car wash. By the end of your first shift, you will see what I mean.

Communications

A skill that I honed while working at Speedee Car Wash was what my wife likes to term my fluency in "mush mouth." Do you barely speak English? Do you talk with an entire pouch of chew in your mouth? Does your vocabulary consist exclusively of slang and obscenities? If so, I can probably understand you as clearly as listening to the guy with the prized voice who does the voiceovers for coming attractions at the movie theatre. By talking to so many people with poor speaking abilities during my years at the car wash, I became accustomed to communicating with all sorts of people. This prepared me very well for my graduate engineering courses, which are more often than not taught by professors for which English is neither their native tongue nor primary priority. While honing my ear to the many perturbations of the English language, my years at the car wash listening to these folks also led me to conclude this: Customers say the darndest things. Here is just a small sampling of those exchanges that stick with me over a decade later.

I had a customer come up to me in the middle of washing his car and mutter, "Ugotainrays?" There were no other words leading up to this utterance to let me tune my ear to his tone or accent, just the single word "ugotainrays."

So I said, "Excuse me? Can you say that again?" I was hoping that the second time I would be ready to hear the words.

Again I heard the single word come flying at me: "Ugotainrays?"

I could tell it was a question from the inflection at the

end, but that was about the extent of what I was picking up from what he was throwing down. I said, "I don't know." (Which was an honest answer.)

Looking confused at *my* answer, the man began to mumble something more substantial. The length of what followed led me to comprehend that whenever this man talked, the mumbled mash that came out of his mouth was not a single word, but rather poorly formed words that flowed seamlessly from one into the next. It was like listening to a foreign language spoken so quickly you cannot make out distinct words. What I did make out from his diatribe was the ending statement of "Ijusneesumrays."

If I was a cartoon character, a light bulb would have appeared above my head. I said, *"Rags!?! You need some rags!?!"*

The man nodded yes and looked relieved that we had established some indication of true communication. The conversation was rather anti-climatic though, because I broke his spirits when I answered, "No." I tried to sell him on the idea of using some Blue Shams as wash rags, but he was not interested.

My sister's favorite question at the car wash was always "Can I get a solid quarter?" This was a foreign expression to the Oliva family when we first opened the car wash. But we were asked it enough through the years that it is evidently a common expression used to distinguish twenty-five cents made up from, say, two dimes and a nickel versus twenty-five cents in the form of a single coin . . . aka "a solid quarter."

I had a guy drive in with Texas license plates on his oversized pickup truck and the heavy Southern drawl to go along with them. This man looked like a walking caricature of a Texan—cowboy boots, cowboy hat, enormous belt buckle, the whole nine yards. He was the only one in the building with me during a summer day. Upon exiting his vehicle, he took one look around and exclaimed, "WoooooooWeeeeee!!!! Never in my LIFE . . . have I been IN an INDOOR car wash!" I wish more of our customers had been that awestruck by our offerings.

In a brief exchange that was funny and creepy at the same time, my sister was once working during summer amid one of the big Harley Davidson reunion events when a couple rode into the car wash—the typical-looking Harley guy and Harley woman on their bike. Jenni went to greet them in their stall, and the guy circled around Jenni eyeing her up and down. He said, "Mmmmm. I'm gonna take you home!" The scary part is that his woman smiled and agreed. (I was not there to witness this, but in my head, when the woman smiled, she did not have any teeth.) Despite their creepy demeanor, they did not hassle Jenni at all and left without incident.

At the time, Jenni did not have a boyfriend, so I told her she should have taken the man up on his offer. For years, if Jenni spoke of meeting a guy somewhere, I would ask, "Did he say 'Mmmm . . . I'm gonna take you home'? Because that is where the bar of affection currently stands."

There was a short period at the car wash in later years when Dad got really pissed that customers were spending so much time in the building and spending so little money. He thus tried to establish a policy that customers had to keep their machines running at all times if they were in the building by feeding quarters into it. If the light on the machine was out, then they better be on their way out the door. This rule change was a disaster, and we on the front lines took the brunt of the fallout. I think Dad eventually abandoned this idea because we all decided we were not going to put up the fight anymore.

If there was anything positive that came out of that short-lived experiment, it was one exclamation of shock from a customer after having had the new rules explained to him. When he fully comprehended them, he yelled, "Even when I'm scrubbin'!?!" This is another phrase that has become part of my family's vernacular for the rest of our lives. It is fun to drop in during showers or dishwashing . . . even if it seems out of context, it still gets a laugh.

A man once drifted in through the front office of Oliva's Garage and encountered Mikey, one of my Dad's mechanics. This guy said to Mikey with no other introduction, "I gotta whuuuh."

Mikey, not knowing what the hell the guy was talking about, took the easy solution and said, "Hold on, I think you need to talk to John for that." So he went back into the garage area and told my father there was a guy who needed to see him.

Dad went to the front office and said, "Hi there. What can I do for you?"

The guy repeated his request of "I gotta whuuh."

Dad said, "Hmmm . . . you gotta whuuh, huh?"

The guy nodded his head and said, "Real bad."

Dad, grasping for anything at this point in the conversation, asked, "Would a bathroom help?"

The guy replied, "Oh yeah."

And with that, Dad showed him to the restroom. Apparently this gentleman had never gotten beyond his preschool years and learned the adult words for poo-poo and pee-pee.

Just a few years back, my wife and I were going on vacation in Mexico. At the airport in Michigan, she stopped at the coffee shop to buy her obligatory third cup of coffee for the day. The coffee shop attendant was an older woman who spoke with a heavy accent. While preparing the drink Lisa ordered, the woman asked, "Uwancova?"

My wife smiled and said, "No thanks, just the coffee."

The courteous woman smiled back and said, "Yeah . . . uwancova?"

Lisa then turned to me and spoke through her smiling teeth like a bad ventriloquist. "What is she asking me???"

I leaned over and said, "She is asking if you want a cover for your coffee."

Lisa quickly responded, "Oohhh!" She then turned to the barista and said, "Yes! I'll take a cover!"

Yeah . . . I've still got it.

Crisis Responses

I suppose one could measure when car wash attendants had paid their dues by a few different milestones. Pulling their first double shifts, their first receipts of physical threats, or the first time a customer tried to get them fired; these were all demented rites of passage at Speedee Car Wash. One item on the list would definitely have to include the first occurrence of an "Oh, my achin' ass" moment. Such moments were characteristic of something truly going wrong at the car wash. Upon learning of the news, my father would grasp his face with both of his hands and mutter, "Oh my achin' ass."

Do you remember the crossbow story? "Oh my achin' ass."

How about the attendant trying to break in through the tiny window in the back door? "Oh my achin' ass."I experienced a few "Oh my achin' ass" events while working at the car wash. (Because our relationship went beyond the confines of the business, I also had a few unrelated to car wash life as well.) The one that sticks in my mind the most was when I had a customer completely blow the paint off of his car.

Given the high-pressure water that we provided and the fact that some of our customers' paint jobs were clinging to the car's surface with just a prayer to begin with, it was not completely unheard of to remove *some* paint from a car's surface. This typically occurred on cars that were already rusting profusely and losing paint when they came in the front door. If slamming your door causes a few chunks of rusted sheet metal to fall to the floor, then you have to foresee that you will lose a bit of paint during the washing too.

However, the car that really set the bar in this category did not fit this customary profile. When it drove in on a quiet Saturday morning, it looked like a run-of-the-mill late model Corvette. It was shiny white and appeared to have a factory-issued paint job. Shortly after the owner began his first wash cycle, he called me over to his stall. I noticed some patches of what looked like thin white plastic lying on the floor. It did not fully register in my head what those patches were until he told me that our car wash was ripping the paint off of his car. He demonstrated by blowing a large patch off in front of me. If this had been me, I would have stopped at the first flake flying off, but this guy continued until about a quarter of the car's paint was on the floor. I called down the street to my father and told him he better come take a walk down the block, because we had taken some paint off a customer's car. Maybe I understated the magnitude of exactly what had occurred, because when Dad walked in the building, I received the "Oh my achin' ass" greeting.

This particular event had some staying power. First the insurance companies got involved, and the case eventually went to court. The car's owner was obviously alleging that our car wash had destroyed his car's paint job, and Speedee Car Wash was arguing that there must have been something faulty with the paint job to begin with. I had no involvement with the case other than receiving the play-by-play from my parents when I got home from school, but my dad had to compile all of this data regarding what pressures and temperatures our water was supplied at, industry standard values, the number of cars we washed on an average day, etc. Through the unfolding of the legal proceedings, it came to light that the car was suffering from a paint delamination phenomenon that plagued many General Motors vehicles of that era. The judge drew the conclusion that since we had been open for over ten years at that point and had safely washed hundreds of thousands of cars, that particular paint job was a lot more suspect in the paint removal than we were.

A lot of employees earned the "Oh my achin' ass" comment by crushing cars. In some cases, this was the result of a simple geometric concept that was lost on the victims. The front door of the building was a standard eight-foot garage door. It was deceiving though, because the first of two speed bumps in the building sat immediately inside the front door. The speed bump was only a few inches high, but to be on the safe side, we always told customers that the front door was only seven-and-a-half feet high. But it did not really matter what we told them, because it turns out that most people driving taller vehicles have no idea how tall their vehicle actually is. This is why so many parking garages and fast-food restaurant drive-thrus have a pipe dangling on chains before their entrance. In other words, they are saying, "We know you don't know how tall your van is, but if you hear a scraping sound when you drive under this bar, it's too tall." That is the vehicular equivalent to "You must be at least this tall to ride this ride."

Speedee Car Wash customers did not have the luxury of the idiot pipe hanging in front of the building, so the first audible warning they received was the metal-on-metal collision between their roof and the steel beam that framed in the garage door opening. Other than a little lost paint, the building always won in these confrontations. Most drivers who were on the verge of violating the height restriction were cognizant enough to realize that they were treading in dangerous waters and appropriately inched their way in. Some bailed at the first onset of contact with the building, resulting in little damage. Others lost their nerve inches before that.

Of course, there were always those customers for which the thought never crossed their minds that they may not fit. Such was the case with the driver of the Holiday Inn courtesy van from down the street. (Incidentally, the Holiday Inn was next door to the Ramada Inn that the rental truck got relocated to in the opening chapter of this book.)

At the time, the Holiday Inn offered its guests transport in a full-size van customized to allow the passengers to move around inside easier by extending the height of the roof. The van was thus a bit taller than a normal van. And the driver had the lack of concern that comes with the territory of driving somebody else's vehicle for a living. Jenni was working the wash the day this guy decided to try to squeeze about eight feet of van through the seven-and-a half-foot opening. He was moving at a pretty good velocity, at least far faster than he should have been if at all worried about height restrictions. So he not only had the height alone working against him but momentum too. Any vehicle bounces up a bit when it hits a speed bump with some forward velocity. With both speed and height working against him, he hit the door frame pretty good. Good enough that the Holiday Inn green stripe is still on the frame today. And I'm sure if that van were still on the road, it too would still have a matching brown stripe from our door frame. When it backed out of the door, it certainly had a noticeable dent that matched the contour of our door. When Dad was called over to witness the aftermath, he undoubtedly uttered, "Oh my achin' ass."

This particular case had little impact on us though. Neither Dad nor the Holiday Inn management bought the attempts of the driver to blame my sister for the incident. At the end of the day, he was the clown behind the wheel. The only aftermath of that episode was that we got a chuckle out of watching the same van and driver drive by the car wash for years to come. Being in such close proximity, we were hard for him to *not* drive past. Even so, it was funny that he never once looked in our direction as he drove by. We were dead to him.

The back door of the building was much taller than the front door, having an opening of twelve feet. But that did not make it any less prone to damaging vehicles. On busy winter days when we had a line of cars down the street waiting to get into the building with both doors closed to keep heat in, coordination of the doors was in the hands of the attendant. To maintain traffic flow, we typically let the exiting customer out the back door, closed the door, then opened the front door to let the next customer in. Having both doors open at the same time was a no-no because the wind and temperature gradient would immediately turn the main aisle into a large wind tunnel, and all of the heat would escape the building. To aid in this door orchestration, the attendant had a remote control for the back door carried on his person. The car wash jackets had a pocket on the left shoulder that held the remote perfectly.

A problem with this setup was the impressive range of the remote. On at least two occasions, attendants were next door in Oliva's Garage's bathroom taking a much needed potty break when they accidently hit the button to close the back door of the car wash. Timing and luck being what it is, these two occasions also coincided with vehicles being under the door at the time it closed. And these commercial grade doors did not have automatic reversing functionality like most home garage doors today.

In a separate incident, a vehicle got crushed in this manner when it exited through the back door, the attendant began to lower the door, and then for whatever reason the customer put the vehicle in reverse and began to come back into the building. "Oh my achin' ass."

On a side note here, there was an entertaining element that came with the height difference between the front and back doors. Even though the back door was much taller, the limit switch on its automatic door opener was set so that the door only opened to a height of eight feet. Regardless, when people with tall vehicles found that they did not fit through the front, they started eying the back door and asked if they could come in through it. Another one of our policies was that *nobody* came in through the back door, because most people cannot drive in reverse, and customers leaving the building were not expecting oncoming traffic, so that was asking for trouble. But since most people would not follow the rule just for the sake of following the rule, we also took to telling people that the back door appearing taller was simply an optical illusion. "No, the two doors are the same height. It's just because that one is farther away, it looks taller." Any kid who has stared down a long highway or a set of railroad tracks disappearing to the horizon knows that as things get farther away, they look smaller. But nobody ever questioned the argument that the back door looked taller because it was farther away.

A far less destructive phenomenon also plagued the door / speed bump system at the other end of vehicle height extremes. We had a large clientele who drove lowriders. Thanks in part to our large Hispanic population of customers, and the popularization of 1964 lowrider Impalas by Dr. Dre and Snoop Doggy Dogg during the 1990s, many Saturdays at the car wash looked like a lowrider car show. I loved working Saturdays for this reason. But a lot of these cars were too low to make it over the speed bumps, which were only a few inches tall. Most just accepted that they were going to scrape on the way in, took it real slow, and dragged concrete for the full length of the car. The guys who had full hydraulics had no problem at all of course. They just raised the car a foot off the ground, pulled into the stall, and dropped the frame on the floor while they washed. Those were awesome. I would ask the guys on their way out to make their cars hop in the building, and they enjoyed having an audience. My dad never appreciated having cars bouncing in the building, but it did not get too out of hand.

Banging up cars was one thing, having attendants get hurt was a whole different matter all together. A lot of us had near misses in terms of almost being hit by cars. Low lighting; foggy, humid air; and lots of people driving around in a relatively small, enclosed space made this unavoidable. But Scott was the only one to ever take a full-on vehicle impact that sent him to the hospital.

The circumstance that led to this episode is the classic tale of an elderly customer getting the brake and accelerator pedals confused while parked in front of the building. There was a line of cars waiting to get in the building. This gentleman had never visited Speedee Car Wash before, so he had parked his car in front of the business, next to the front door. After talking to Scott about how the operation worked, he got back into his car, and Scott walked through the personnel access door that is just to the north of the drive-through door. This is the point at which the man was trying to back out of the parking lot when he put the car in drive instead of reverse, panicked when the car began moving in the wrong direction, and hit the gas instead of the brake. "Oh my achin' ass." The lower part of Scott's leg got pinched between the building and the car. The door and frame got damaged enough that they had to be replaced, and Scott wound up with a broken bone in his foot. He was wearing steel-toe boots, so the injuries could have been much more severe. If nothing else good came of the event, Scott at least got the most legit war story out of it from his car wash days.

The strangest collision that happened at the business did not involve anybody getting hurt. It did not even involve a driver for that matter. For a brief period, the car wash had a Pepsi machine in front of it. (It only survived a year or two.) Scott was working one weekend when he heard a crash in front of the building. He walked out to find that a car had smashed into the Pepsi machine, completely destroying it. The crumpled machine had acted as an excellent energy absorber; the building came away unscathed except for a few minor scratches. But there was no driver to be seen, and in fact, the car was locked and not running. It took awhile to piece together what happened, but it turns out that the car had been parked in the lot of the apartments across the street. The owner had left the car in neutral, and something eventually caused it to start rolling down the apartment driveway, across the street, and into our parking lot where the Pepsi machine put an end to its self-guided joy ride. "Oh my achin' ass." That whole occurrence still seems rather hard to believe for me. The two driveways are not directly across the street from one another, so the car had to navigate at least two turns to reach its final destination. Even if it were instead parked on the street, it still had to make one turn into our parking lot. And it had to cross four lanes of Thirteenth Street without hitting any vehicles. But what other explanation could there be? Did somebody hate Pepsi so much that they sacrificed their own vehicle to take out a vending machine?

And the final absurd collision story comes from earlier in the car wash's history, when we were still living right next door to the business. We had gotten one of those tacky light-up signs with an arrow of light bulbs across the top, and four rows of plastic tracks in which letters can be arranged to display a message. The sign was advertising the car wash and garage, but it sat on the front lawn of our house, which was a few feet higher in elevation than the parking lots of the business.

One night my parents awoke to a commotion outside their bedroom. A drunk driver had driven across the front lawn of our house, first taking out the sign, then a bush that was planted in our yard, and finally coming to rest against our neighbor's building. He had come only feet from hitting the front of our house.

The sign was completely bent to hell and worthless after that incident. In typical Dad fashion though, he righted the mangled heap of twisted metal, broken plastic, and shattered light bulbs. On a few lines of the reader board that could still manage to hold letters, he displayed one final message to passing motorists: "THIS SIGN FOR RENT." Say it with me . . . "Oh my achin' ass."

Legacy

I mentioned already that during my short professional career, I have already had more than my fair share of different jobs. From this statement, it can be rightly inferred that I have had to resign from more than my fair share number of jobs as well. (Thankfully I can say that I have left every job thus far by my own choice. In today's volatile world economy, I am very aware of those not as fortunate in this employment lottery. There are too many out there who cannot say the same through no fault of their own.) Submitting a resignation letter never ceases to instill fear in me like no other life event. I do not know why this is. But every time I walk into my boss's office and announce that I have decided to take another position, I always stress out about the task days beforehand. And when the moment finally arrives, I don my beat-dog persona, fully expecting my manager to haul off and deck me. Such a reaction has not happened yet, but in this case, avoidance of this reaction in the past has not instilled any confidence of future avoidances.

It is thus logical that walking away from my lucrative employment at Speedee Car Wash should have created the greatest level of anxiety within me as my tenure was about to come to a close. Sure, at some level, from day one it was always understood that the car wash was just a temporary gig until I finished school. However, even with that in the back of my mind, the self-serving idea that I would be abandoning my father and my family to run the family business in my absence was all too real.

Perhaps my view that I had become a critical cog in the machine that was Speedee Car Wash was not that overstated.

By the time I was a senior in college, the academic year of 1998-1999, I was one of the last stable employees left attending the car wash. My sister had finished her master's degree a year earlier and moved on to the first full-time position of her professional life. Scott had also graduated from the technical college he had been attending and was working as an apprentice at a tool and die shop . . . the first step toward earning his Journey Man's card. For the most part, I was the only regular attendant left.

With the advantage of hindsight and maturity on my side now, I do not know how I failed to foresee the inevitable. By the time fall faded into winter, the car wash's hours were no longer maintaining the regularity that they had for the previous fifteen years. When my class schedule allowed, I would be at the wash during the week. Similarly, if my dad did not have a lot of repair work coming through the garage, he would go next door and open the car wash. But barring those two circumstances, the business remained closed. Customers asked me why we were keeping such haphazard hours. I did not have an answer. I often asked Dad if he was going to start looking for some new attendants and gently reminded him that in less than a half of a year, I too would be graduating and hopefully moving on to bigger and better things. He just blew me off or avoided the question all together.

As that winter began, right around the Christmas and New Year's holidays, we had a frigid streak of cold weather in Milwaukee. High temperatures hovered around the teens and single digits for weeks. Just like years before, we did not bother opening the business on *really* cold days. We could lose a day's worth of profits by just opening the overhead doors once and letting all of the heat escape from the building. So our temporary weather delay came as no surprise to me.

After we got into the year 1999, it took until the middle of January for the weather to rebound out of its bitterly cold temperatures. The first Saturday after the thermal recovery,

I was shocked that my dad told me we would not be opening the car wash that day. I asked why, and again he did not provide a direct response. That weekend passed, as did the next, without washing a single car. As was the norm, our mutual frustration or anger manifested itself in silence. A couple weeks later, I finally confronted my father and demanded to know what the hell was going on. He finally stated the obvious . . . he had no intentions of reopening the car wash ever again. He had had enough; he was done.

Selfishly, I was upset. I was out of a job. I had roughly five months of school left, and I was already feverishly applying for engineering jobs to begin after graduation. There was no way I was going to find some other part-time job to fill in the short gap. I don't think I fully appreciated my father's utter exhaustion at the time. I had been on the frontlines of the car wash wars for about seven years at that point. Dad had been doing it for almost thirty. He was tired of it. Now I look back and wonder how he lasted for so long. But my parents had stuck to their word: Throughout high school and college, my sister and I always had a job at Speedee Car Wash, and neither of us had to succumb to working in the fast food industry.

An often said adage is "You can't go home." I believe that, on some levels, this resonates more with me than with others. After graduation, it became clear that the entry level engineering job I was hoping for would not be coming my way. I then defaulted to my unofficial "Plan B," which was to enroll in graduate school to pursue my master's degree. At the time, this seemed like a total surrendering, so I was running to grad school with my tail between my legs. Time has demonstrated though that it was a good decision, and I would do it again. By the fall of 1999, I had moved to Flint, Michigan, and was enrolled in Kettering University's graduate school.

Within just a year after Speedee Car Wash closing its

doors for the final time, going home was already not a trip back to where I had grown up. The car wash was permanently closed, standing as a haunting memory to what was. My sister and I had moved on to the next stages of our careers. And devastatingly, Scott had committed suicide. Even Martino's paved over their miniature golf course and put a parking lot in its place shortly after I left town.

While the three of us had worked at the car wash side by side for all of those years, we sometimes speculated on what the future would hold for both us and Speedee Car Wash. Would the next generation of car wash employees even know who we were? Would they be told celebrated tales of when John's kids and nephew manned the stalls? Would we become legendary characters like those employees who went before us? Would Dad let us come back on a busy weekend in winter and relive our glory days, donning the grimy car wash jackets of our youth? Within too short of a time period, these questions bluntly answered themselves.

Aside from all of the anecdotal "lessons" that took place during my time at the car wash, I also feel that I left there having learned some things greater than any formal education has provided me since. On the surface, one could observe how my father treated customers and conclude that he was a heartless, sarcastic, uncaring person. But I think that is a superficial judgment. I think that after years of watching him interact with people, I have found that he has more of a Robin-Hood-like approach to the public. Instead of stealing from the rich and giving to the poor, he hassles the "powerful" and helps out the underdog. In this context, the powerful are those who perceive themselves as having the upper hand, the self-importance that comes with wealth, social stature, corporate rank, or any other fictitious means of leverage that our culture endows upon the often unworthy. They came into our business and expected us to bow down to their stature just like much of the rest of society did. Dad was there to remind them that, at least in that one building, he was in charge, and they were going to play by his rules.

On the other side of the spectrum, I saw my dad help countless people who had shaken a bad role of the dice in the game of life. This in part explains why some of Speedee Car Wash's employees were such a ragtag motley crew. Ex-convicts, the uneducated, the chronically unemployed, war veterans struggling to find their way . . . the characters that the rest of society were quick to dismiss as losers, Dad was willing to give a chance to, to enable them to earn an honest day's wage. A lot of this population proved to be an unworthy cause, but that did not deter Dad from trying to help the next case that emerged. And we all hoped that the car wash was a stepping stone on the way up, not a destination in itself.

A non-car-wash related story that speaks to this happened during my tenure at the car wash. My mom had once-a-month meetings for her job that required her to stay at work late. This left me and Dad to fend for ourselves for dinner, which usually meant fast food. On one such occasion, we were walking into a local Hardees restaurant when Dad was stopped by a guy in the parking lot. This individual said, "Hey, man, how's it going? Do you have any cash I can borrow? I'm really hungry."

Dad continued the conversation with the man's same casual tone. From the familiarity in this exchange, I just assumed they knew each other. Dad said, "No, I don't have any cash, but my son and I were about to go in the restaurant here. If you're hungry, come in and we'll get you something to eat."

At this point, I'm thinking, *Oh great, I get to eat dinner with this guy.* So, we went in, and we all told the cashier what we wanted to eat. The guy got his food, thanked Dad with a handshake, and walked out the door. As we sat down to eat, I asked Dad who the guy was. I was shocked when Dad said, "I don't know . . . apparently some hungry guy."

I told Dad that I thought he knew him, and he just

said, "Nope . . . never saw the guy before in my life." It was exchanges like this that had a lasting impression on me.

In a similar event, when I had moved to Flint, Michigan, for grad school, we were walking into a local church for Sunday morning mass when a guy approached Dad and said, "Hey! How's it going!?! I haven't seen you since we both worked on the line at the GM assembly plant!" They caught up on old times for a bit and exchanged what each was up to now in their current lives. When Dad joined us in the pew, he once again told me that he had no idea who the guy was . . . but he did not want to crush the guy's spirits, so he just went along with it.

In my days since leaving the car wash, I have continued to see different facets of this never ending battle between the blue collar working class and the white collar executive class, and in many ways, I feel caught somewhere in between, not knowing which side of the war I am actually on. It's funny, when I worked at the car wash, people just concluded that I was a burned out high school dropout destined to work at a car wash for the rest of my life. They treated me with the same lack of respect that the ruling class of medieval times regarded the peasants. Now that I have managed to rise above my car wash attending days, and I get paid to sit in an office rather than perform manual labor, I sense the resentment from those in my presence who still "work" for a living, doing something more physical to earn their keep. As an engineer, I interact with many trades people, such as welders, machinists, plumbers, and the like. Too many of them are quick to assume that here is this stuffed shirt who was born with a silver spoon in his mouth and has never worked a real day in his life. And now that I have earned my doctorate, even within the ranks of other college graduates I find this same phenomenon. Those engineers I work with who stopped their academic education at a bachelor's degree look at me from the same perspective as the trades people. They are somehow more genuine and down to earth than the almighty PhD holder. But the medical doctors are still around to remind me that I am not a "real doctor." I guess it is just human nature to find comfort in thinking that you are better off than some people, while feeling inferior to others, for whatever reason.

About two years after the car wash closed, I made mention to my parents that if they had any official Speedee Car Wash jackets remaining, I would like to have one. It would serve as a memento of where I had come from and the times we had. I thought I remembered that they had just bought a few new jackets when the business shut down.

To my delight, that year for Christmas, not only did I receive a brand new car wash jacket that had never seen active duty, but I had risen to the ranks that I merited a personalized model! On the left side chest, embroidered in scripted yellow letters was "John." Owing to my Father's typical warped sense of humor, the right side of the coat had four embroidered letters in a block font: "MFIC." When I asked Dad what "MFIC" was, he smirked and said, "That was your title . . . the Mother Fucker In Charge." I am proud to say that, because of this coat, there are some circles where I am known simply as "The MFIC." Like the tales of Elvis watching football on Sundays sitting in his Graceland living room in full football uniform and pads, I have been known to throw on my Speedee Car Wash jacket and head to a local self-serve car wash to wash one of my own vehicles or my wife's. Call me a purist, but I still prefer the simpler car washes versus the more elaborate and modernized renditions. There is nothing more nostalgic for this ex-attendant than dropping quarters into a box and hearing the pressurized wand kick on. (Since I rarely have any cash on me, I do appreciate these new fangled self-service car washes that have credit card slots on the machines. I can only imagine what headaches those must cause! Another modern development is that I have found that the arm pocket on the car wash jacket that used to hold the door remote is now very convenient for holding a cell phone.)

I also recently acquired the last remaining stock of Blue Shams that Speedee Car Wash had on hand when it closed its doors, so I should be well equipped to dry for a few years to come as well. I am still waiting for somebody to see my jacket and approach me asking me to make change. And I might just kick over a bucket or two for old time sake. I have not yet found another wash that has attendants, but if I do, maybe I'll become a Ron-like customer and spend my Saturday mornings telling stories of the good old days at The Car Wash.

Epilogue

Using a self-service car wash, especially one as simplistic as Speedee Car Wash seems to be an obviously simple task. But, like with anything else, spending years watching the same activity allowed me to pick up subtle nuances of the game. I have thus compiled a list of helpful hints for any of you who may find yourself navigating the local coin-op car wash.

1. Use the foaming brush—A high-pressure power washing is good for removing large pieces of debris, dead bugs, mud, and snow. Road grime, though—that hard-to-classify film coating on a dirty car's surface—is pretty resilient to pressure washing. The most effective means of removing road grime requires some physical contact—sponge, rag, or foaming brush. Without a source of mechanical contact between the grime and the painted surface of the car, there is not great enough force to break the electrostatic attraction between them. If you want to test this theory, wash half of your car using only pressurized water and use something to scrub the surface on the other half. Once you get your car out into the sunlight, you will see a definitive line between the two sides. (This works best on dark cars.) Or you can take my word for it . . . I have done the experiment myself. In a moment of utter boredom once at the car wash, I read an issue of one of the many professional car washing trade magazines that my father received in the mail. It contained an article that addressed this very point. The author was discussing the touchless automatic wash bays. Often, one or two of these accompany a traditional self-serve car wash. It is very similar to the self-serve bay, but it is an entirely automated machine that circles the car and spray washes the vehicle with mechanized equipment. The article said something on the order of "A touchless automatic has never really gotten a car clean, but the American public loves them anyway."

2. Wash the foaming brush before you use it—Most car washes that I have visited have a note near the foaming brush that the customers should wash off the brush head with the pressure wand before using the brush. I can also say from years of observation that most car wash patrons do not heed this advice. The point is that the brush itself is designed to be soft and not harm your car's finish. You don't know what the asshole in front of you did with that brush though. If the previous customer had a very muddy vehicle, the brush can be imbedded with dirt and pebbles. Worse yet, when people scrub their wheels with the brush, abrasive brake dust gets all over the brush. If this is the case, you might as well scrub your car with a piece of steel wool.

3. Do not forget your floor mats—At Speedee Carwash, we had various collections of things commonly left behind by people—sponges, contraband buckets, towels, etc. But the most commonly left items were floor mats. Whether taking them out of the vehicle to vacuum beneath them or removing them to pressure wash them, people were always forgetting their floor mats. We accumulated a pile a couple feet tall that stood next to the door to the north pump room. Depending on our mood, we might sell them to inquiring customers for a couple bucks a piece too.

4. Opt for a stall closer to the pump room—When you pull into your local car wash, get a feel for how the facility is laid out, and if available, take a stall as close to the pump room as possible. Pressure drop, temperature drop, and time to change between different wash fluids all become worse the farther you are from the pumps and fluid sources.

5. Read signs—By getting this far in this book, you have already read more than the average American does on an annual basis. But don't stop at books! Information in the form of the printed word is everywhere, especially at an unattended self-service car wash. Take two or three minutes during your next visit to read all of the signs in a given wash bay and on the front of the building if applicable. You might just learn something that will benefit every visit you make there in the future.

6. Do not underestimate the power of the vacuums—Don't be the dumbass who has to say, "Your vacuums suck." Treat the sucking power of the vacuum with respect. Watch where you point the business end of that thing. If there is any question in your mind, such as, I wonder if the vacuum is strong enough to suck up my car keys, just assume that it is.

7. Do not underestimate the power of high-pressure water—At close range, the water pressure coming out of the spray wands at a self-service car wash can do real damage. It can blow a hole through the palm of your hand, and we have demonstrated that given the right conditions, it can rip the paint job off your car. But if you hold the tip at least a foot from any target, the pressure will have subsided to a safe level before coming in contact with the object.

8. Check that your quarters are actually quarters—You cheap bastards, stop trying to skimp on twenty-five cents by sticking video game tokens and electrical box knock outs in the machines. The monetary savings is not worth the embarrassment of getting caught.

9. Do not drop anything down the sewer—With rare exception, the sewer grate should be treated as a one-way passage. Lots goes in, little comes out. And searching for something that went in is a futile exercise.

10. If you have any suspicion that your vehicle is too tall to fit beneath an obstacle, don't try!— Most households have a device called a "tape measure." On a nice flat surface, park your jacked up redneck pickup, oversized RV, or contractor van with twenty ladders on top of it. Then place a flat board or piece of cardboard at the highest point on the vehicle and use the tape measure to measure the distance between the bottom of the board and the surface of the ground. If you do not know where the highest point on your vehicle is, take several measurements at different positions and retain the largest value as the accepted height of your vehicle. With this number in hand, you will no longer need to take advantage of the idiot pipes hanging around the country.

11. Do not piss off the car wash attendant—They have spent a lot longer playing this game than you have. They will get their way one way or the other. So, please, keep the car wash attendant happy by following their seemingly simple rules, and try not to make their existence any crappier than it already is. And don't try to get them fired. For all you know, you may already be dealing with the good cop in that car wash's good cop / bad cop hierarchy.

CPSIA information can be obtained at www.ICGtesting.com
Printed in the USA
BVOW081433260313

316384BV00006B/6/P